NIIHAU

*The Traditions
of a
Hawaiian Island*

Passage through a fresh water pond. (*Photo: Bishop Museum*)

NIIHAU

MOKU O KAHELELANI

*Island of the Chief Kahelelani
Great Chief of Niihau
Ten generations ago*

Village of Puuwai, Island of Niihau. (*Photo: Bishop Museum*)

NIIHAU

The Traditions of a Hawaiian Island

Rerioterai Tava
Moses K. Keale, Sr.

Mutual Publishing

CREDITS:
Editing: Glen Grant
Design: Momi Cazimero
Cover design: Gonzalez Design
Computer production: Andrea Hines, Scott Rutherford
Map illustration: Scott Rutherford

Proverbs of Mary Kawena Pukui reprinted from *'Ōlelo No'eau: Hawaiian Proverbs and Poetical Sayings* by Mary Kawena Pukui, published as B.P. Bishop Museum Special Publication 71. Copyright by Bishop Museum 1983. Used by permission. And from *Hula: Historical Perspectives* by Dorothy B. Barrère, Mary Kawena Pukui & Marion Kelly, published as Pacific Anthropological Records 30. Copyright by Bishop Museum 1980. Used by permission.

© 1989 by Mutual Publishing

Third Printing, August 2006

Text © 1984 by Rerioterai Tava and Moses Kapalekilahao Keale, Sr.

All rights reserved.

No part of this book may be reproduced in any form or by any electronic or mechanical means, including information storage and retrieval devices or systems, without prior written permission from the publisher, except that brief passages may be quoted for review.

LCC 88-061419
ISBN-10: 0-935180-80-X
ISBN-13: 978-0-935180-80-0

Mutual Publishing, LLC
1215 Center Street, Suite 210
Honolulu, Hawai'i 96816
Ph: 808-732-1709 / Fax: 808-734-4094
email: mutual@mutualpublishing.com
www.mutualpublishing.com

Printed in Korea

Aina Nui o Niihau
piliwale mai o Lehua.

Great is the land of Niihau
and Lehua is nearby.

Aina pohaku o Puukole
ika ehukai
ika nou halaole ake Koolau.

A land of rock is Puukole
in the salt spray
pelting without missing the Koolau.

Aina o Kaula ike komohana
hoa paio no ke Konahea.

The island of Kaula lies to the west
an opponent of the Konahea winds.

—Olelo Noeau, *by Mary Pukui*

TABLE OF CONTENTS

Foreword . . . . *xi*
Acknowledgments . . . . *xii*
Preface . . . . *xiii*
Brief Facts about Niihau . . . . *xv*
List of Photographs . . . . *xvi*
List of Mele . . . . *xvii*

Chapter I	Niihau: An Island Caressed by Time	1
Chapter II	The Sacred Days of Old on Niihau	9
Chapter III	Ka Poe Kahiko — The People of Old	23
Chapter IV	Niihau After Captain Cook	43
Chapter V	The Way of Life on Niihau	57
Chapter VI	Myths and Legends of Heroes and Demigods	69
Chapter VII	Place Names of Niihau	81
Chapter VIII	Place Names of Lehua, Kaula and Nihoa	97

Afterword 105

Appendices

A. List of Residents of Nihoa on March 7, 1884 107
B. Letters to the Minister of the Interior in 1863 and 1864 108
   Niihau family names during the 1800s 109
C. Royal Patent 111
D. Moena Pawehe Designs 112

Glossary 115
Bibliography 119
Map Index and Map 121
Index 133

Olelo Hai Mua

*H*E MOOLELO KUPA keia e pili ana no Niihau, oiahoi o Niihau Moku o Kahelelani mai ka wa o kona nohoalii ana ma ia moku a hiki i keia au nei. Na Kahelelani me kana mau kaukaualii i hookaulana ia Niihau a me na makaainana o ia moku ma kahi o umikumamaono hanauna mamua aku nei.

Pono kakou, e na poe e heluhelu ana i keia moolelo kupa no Niihau, e hoomahalo ia Rerioterai Tava a me Moses Kapalekilahao Keale, Makua, i ko laua hoolaulima ana i hiki e hoike a e hoolaha i keia moolelo no Niihau. Ehiku makahiki a oi ko laua noi ana i loaa a e hookuio i na mea i palapala ia iloko o keia moolelo kupa no Niihau i na hanuna ua hala akula a hiki i keia hanauna nei.

Eia kekahi mea hoihoi i hookomo pu ia i keia moolelo kupa, oiahoi, he mau kope o na palapala o Ke Aupuni Moi Hawaii pili i ke kuai hoolilo ana o Niihau i ka ohana Sinclair. Ma keia mau palapala e ike pono aku kakou na mea kuio pili i ke kuai ana o ia moku.

Hookahi mea ahuwale koe, oiahoi, he mea pili ana i ka pai ole ana o na kahako a me na okina i keia paiana. He mau mea loii i ke ao ana o ka olelo Hawaii auanei. Aka he kumunoonoo pono keia no keia wa, Kupono ka pai ole o ia mau kiko hookalelo leo anei no ka mea kupaa mau na lau kanaka ma Niihau i ka hoohana ole o na kahako a me na okina i ko lakou kakau ana.

A. K. PIIANAIA

FOREWORD

*T*HIS IS A COLLECTION OF TRADITIONS belonging to Niihau, that is, the Niihau of Kahelelani, from the time of his rule to the present. It was Kahelelani and his supporting chieftains who brought renown to Niihau and its inhabitants beginning about sixteen generations ago.

It is proper for us who read this native collection of traditions to acknowledge with deep gratitude, Rerioterai Tava, of Tahitian descent now residing on Oahu, and Moses Kapalekilahao Keale Sr., a native Niihauan now residing on Kauai, for having collaborated in their efforts to bring to the public's attention these traditions of Niihau. For seven years they worked at collecting, identifying and translating these records of the people of Niihau.

Among the interesting items incorporated in this collection of traditions are copies of the documents of the true Hawaiian Kingdom that recorded the sale of Niihau to the Sinclair family. Through these documents one can see the truth about the island. Finally, one item remains which may illicit criticism from contemporary teachers of the Hawaiian language—the conspicuous absence of macrons and glottol stops in Hawaiian words. It was the writers' decision not to use these in their work on Niihau for the simple reason that the people of Niihau do not use them in their writing. I support and salute them on their decision in this matter.

A. K. PIIANAIA, Director of Hawaiian Studies
University of Hawaii at Manoa
August 25, 1987
Olelo Hai Mua

*A*CKNOWLEDGMENTS

*T*HE VALUE of collecting Niihau's oral history and tradition reaches beyond the academic merit of such a collection. The preservation of this will be matched only by the respect and pride that the younger generations will receive from the traditions, legends and heritage of the island that have been lost to them for so long. To them we dedicate this book.

This book has been many years in preparation and we are indebted to many people for their kind assistance. Our *mahalo nui loa* to all those who shared their special knowledge with us about life on Niihau, then and now. Some of the information within this book may conflict with other theories from the outside world, but these have been passed down generation to generation without the benefit of museums, libraries or archives. The information, however, has been supplemented with facts from published sources whenever possible.

The Niihau ledgers were all written in the Hawaiian language, as were some of the taped interviews. The Hawaiian was translated into English by a true son of Niihau, Moses Kapalekilahao Keale Sr. Based on his work and other sources, Rerioterai Tava, a daughter of Tahiti, wrote the book.

To the staff of the Bishop Museum, Hawaii State Archives and the Hawaiian Mission Children's Society Library, thank you for all of your assistance. Special appreciation goes to Eleanor Williamson of the Bishop Museum who gave encouragement and, graciously, her time and critique. Mahalo to Laura Kamalani, our typist, and Glen Grant, editor, who gave this work their personal attention. We are most grateful to the *kupuna* of Niihau for their fierce pride in the traditions, customs and heritage of their island. *Me ke aloha o ka haku o Iesu Kristo me kakou, amene.*

There remain still unprinted stories and legends that we hope to include in the next book, for the culture belongs to the people.

Aloha ke Akua,

Rerioterai Tava
Moses Kapalekilahao Keale Sr.

PREFACE

TO DATE, very little has been written about Niihau. History books devote barely half a page to it; legends are scanty; information on lifestyle and culture is shrouded in mystery. Yet, this island, seventh largest in the Hawaiian chain, is teeming with history and legend. The isolation encouraged by the owners has preserved its people from the ills of modern civilization. If there is any place left in the world where the culture of the Hawaiian Islands still persists intact, it is certainly here on Niihau.

The elders of Niihau are afraid that the younger generation will forget their heritage and culture as time goes by and as they become inevitably absorbed into the lifestyles of contemporary Hawaii. The elders are keenly aware that Niihau is the *last* place where Hawaiian culture *lives*. The Robinsons have tried to protect the people and their culture by occasionally imposing laws upon them that many "modern people" would find hard to accept. Some outside observers, unable to understand the value of this near-perfect kind of life, feel compelled to try and change it.

This collection of history, lore and anecdotes concerning Niihau is intended as a record of the older way of life through 1982 when the work was initiated. The material is presented so that the knowledge of the island people will not be forgotten. By sharing the story of Niihau as told by its own residents, the culture and history of this unique place will be perpetuated for the existing younger generation and for generations yet to come.

Most the of the information in this book comes from old Niihau Hawaiian ledgers kept by the islanders, and from interviews with elders, especially Tutu Kaui (Keola Kauileilehua Keamoai). Born on Niihau on January 30, 1912, Kaui's original name was Ka-ui o Lehua, "the beauty of Lehua," but *Kauileilehua* was mistakenly written on his birth registration. He served as a knowledgeable bridge to the days of old.

Kaui married Victoria Kanahele and they had five children. Tutu Kaui left Niihau for work on Kauai in 1930. He was severely injured in an accident that left him paralyzed from the waist down. As a youngster he rode along with his grandfather and father as they did their work. While resting, stories were told of the "ole days". Tutu was very interested and retained most of the information. Today he is remembered as the most knowledgeable *kupuna*. He died on June 7, 1988.

An explanation about the use of the Hawaiian language in this work will be helpful. Many of the new works of the Hawaiian linguists contain diacritical marks. However, we have chosen not to use them here as most of the Niihau ledgers used as sources do not contain them and to insert them could change the whole connotation of a word or name. On many occasions, we have replaced the letter "K" with the letter "T," to more closely correspond to the manner of speech on Niihau, which remains true to the original ancestral language. Also, the reader will sometimes note different spellings of some words, for instance, "Kauwai" for "Kauai," "Uwala" for "Uala," et cetera; they appear here just as they were written in the Niihau ledgers. In addition, some of the Hawaiian words or their spellings are unique to Niihau. These have been noted in italics in the glossary.

Many of the stories here are based on historical events or natural phenomena; some combine fiction and fact. They were told by Hawaiians speaking *as* Hawaiians, like Tutu Kaui, who told some stories and confirmed others, true in spirit and thought as he remembered hearing them from childhood through adulthood. The stories related here are told in a manner that preserves the original Hawaiian thought and mode of expression. Past and present often merge—Western notions of "objective fact" sometimes succumb to the richer Hawaiian subjective insight.

In some cases, it was not possible to translate *mele* due to conflicting information in the oral accounts.

The Hawaiians had an unwritten literature at which chosen persons were highly skilled. These preservers of culture were so in tune with nature that their eyes, ears and minds were exceptionally well-developed. Some of the stories related here are termed "mythical," others are never questioned as factual. Regardless, the stories have a deep hold on the people of Niihau. Niihau is so interwoven with fact and fancy, history and legend, it becomes hard to tell where one begins and the other ends. Tutu Kaui said, "Call it what you wish . . . but many of these I have seen to be true."

THE ISLAND OF NIIHAU

Distance from Honolulu
152 statute miles

Total land area
Niihau, 47,217 acres • Lehua Island, 291 acres

Size
18 miles by 6 miles

Population
226

Highest point
Paniau, at 1,281 feet above sea level

Mean altitude
530 feet

Economic activities
Fishing, sheep ranching, charcoal production, honey cultivation

Inland lakes
Lake Halulu, 182 acres • Lake Halalii, 841 acres

LIST OF PHOTOGRAPHS

Fresh water pond	*ii*
Village of Puuwai	*iv*
Kaunuapua Heiau	10
Demonstration of hei *(cat's cradle)*	24
Aerial photograph of Kaumuhonu Bay	44
Iubile Church	56
Village homes	58
Fishing from canoes	68
Keanaoku, home of the shark guardian	70
Central Plateau	82
Cave shelters on Nihoa	98
School children, Puuwai	106
Moena Pawehe, makaloa mat	114

LIST OF MELE

Aloha Niihau — Moena Pawehe Hula 19
Mele of the Winds on Niihau 30
Pupu o Niihau 37
Puuone 39
Ka Hui Nalu 40
Hosana 50
Na Ia Ono o Ka Aina 65
Traditional Song 83
Mele No Na Pali 87

CHAPTER I

An Island Caressed by Time

*Puuwai kau mai iluna
hooheno ia nei e ka ua naulu*

Looking up to Puuwai
caressed by the rains of the Naulu

An Island Caressed by Time I 3

*F*OR MORE than a century, the Hawaiian island of Niihau has been forbidden to outsiders. The owners are the Robinson family, descendants of the Sinclairs who originally purchased the island in 1864. Keeping the privacy of Niihau as a way to protect the Hawaiian lifestyles of the residents, the Robinson family has restricted visits over the years to an occasional invited guest, a few public officials and physicians. To add to the mystique of life there, the family will not grant any interviews to discuss aspects of life on Niihau. Most information about the people and their lifestyles has been gathered from Niihau residents themselves.

According to the 1980 census, there were 226 persons living on Niihau. Approximately two thirds of the residents are Hawaiian, comprising the largest colony of pure Hawaiians in the state. The remaining part-Hawaiian residents are a mixture of Japanese, Portuguese, Chinese or other ancestry. The Niihauans are free to travel to and from the island whenever they wish. What little information that outsiders have received suggests that the lifestyle of Niihau retains a special native Hawaiian spirit that resembles the rural Hawaii of a fading past.

The physical remoteness of Niihau from mainstream Oahu life contributes to this sense of time standing still. Situated 17.5 miles southwest of Kauai, Niihau is believed to be the oldest of the eight major islands in the Hawaiian chain—it's age is estimated to be five to seven million years old. Seventh in size in the Hawaiian chain, it is relatively small—the island comprises seventy-two square miles and is approximately eighteen miles long and eight miles across at its widest point. It is shaped something like a foot. Of the island's 47,217 acres, 46,705 acres are privately owned. The state and federal government each own 256 acres of land, which was ceded either by presidential proclamation or governor's executive order. In 1983, the State Department of Taxation assessed the value of the entire island at $7.20 an acre.

The island of Niihau is a remnant of a once-substantial shield volcano. Geological evidence suggests that the volcano's summit was at a point about a mile or so east of the present island, and that the ocean eroded most of the ancient volcano peak, particularly from the east side. Some experts believe that the disappearance of much of the shield's eastern side was due to vertical faulting. Should this be true, a substantial portion of the volcano separated and slowly sank into the ocean, leaving only one side to form the low mountains that are on the east side of Niihau. Volcanic cones stand at each end of the island: Kawaihoa at the southern tip and Lehua, now an island, at the northern end. Both *aa* and *pahoehoe* lava are found on Niihau. Niihau rises 13,000 feet above the ocean floor—the highest point above sea level is 1,281 feet at Paniau, although seventy-eight percent of Niihau is less than 500 feet in elevation.

Niihau has a coastline of 200 miles, of which 110 miles are prone to tidal-wave action. The coastline terrain can be quite dramatic—there are three miles of sea cliffs of 1,000-foot elevation or more. The fringing reef to the north and south of the island is, in many areas, exposed at the sea's surface. Some of these limestone masses are residuals of large size that were islands when the reef was growing around the island. Beaches on the east shore collect ocean debris and are dotted with glass Japanese fishing "balls," or floats—now a rarity elsewhere.

An extensive geological survey of Niihau conducted in 1921 by Norman E. A. Hinds indicated a significant submerged mountain and a bench or reef ledge. Dr. Hinds received permission from Niihau's owner, Aubry Robinson, to conduct an eight-day study of the island, collecting fossils and making offshore soundings. From these studies he concluded that the mountain forming Niihau is mostly submerged, with its base 2,000 to 2,500 fathoms deep (a depth which makes further study difficult). Judging from the present sea cliffs, he suggested that Niihau must have originally been forty miles in diameter; today, wind, rain, wave erosion and downward faulting have reduced the island to less than thirty-two miles in diameter. More than half of the eastern six miles of land is now also submerged. Soundings conducted 1.5 miles off the southern point of Niihau showed a submerged reef ledge forty fathoms deep. Another reef shelf sixty feet below sea level was found to extend eastward six more miles.

The land features of the island are also diverse. There are essentially four types of geography, each in equal parts: mountain range, pastureland, marginal pastureland that is fertile only during the rainy months and sand, rocks and ponds. The uplands and most of the pastureland are covered with five feet of rich red dirt, which is common in old volcanic lands. The southwest coast has cemented sand dunes up to 150 feet high. Of Niihau's seventy-three square miles, sixty-nine are dry land or temporarily and partially covered by water. Niihau has an arid climate. The high mountains of Kauai block rain clouds from reaching Niihau. In addition, the island's low elevation causes little precipitation. In fact, the island gets so little rain that there are no permanent forests. Despite the aridity, there are 3.4 square miles of permanent water, lakes and reservoirs. Niihau also has the largest natural lake in the state, Lake Halulu, which comprises 182 acres. A U.S. Geological Survey in the 1920s documented the presence of about fifty freshwater *punawai*. There may be others that are hidden or secret.

Puuwai is Niihau's principle town or settlement. The original name of the settlement was Kauanaulu. However, when another church was opened at Kauanaulu, the name of the town was changed to *Puuwai Aloha o ka Ohana*. With time, it was shortened to simply Puuwai.

The manner of life on Niihau today has not changed much since the turn of the century—a unique rural setting has been preserved that might well be envied by some discontents of modern life. Life simply moves more slowly on Niihau. It was believed by many in the days of old and remains true today: Niihauans are superior in many ways to other Hawaiian islanders. They are hard working, sober and well-taken care of. Idleness is rare, and free time is spent sharing life with friends and family. They live off the produce of the land, relying only on a few store-bought foods. Transportation is by bicycle or walking; sometimes horses, which are owned by the Robinsons, are used by the cowboys. The serenity of this island paradise is disturbed only by the frequent screeching of peacocks.

> *Puuwai kau mai iluna, hooheno ia nei e ka ua naulu* — "Looking up to Puuwai, caressed by the rain of the *naulu* wind."

The town of Puuwai is a picturesque scene of small houses, quiet roads and the church. The homes are widely scattered throughout the town amid large *kiawe* trees, cactus and rocks. There is a short main street approximately three-quarters of a mile in length. Many of the homes are more than 1,000 feet apart from each other. Each home is surrounded by a rock wall that forms a private yard, which is used mostly to keep out the sheep and pigs. Many of the rock walls are covered with night-blooming cereus, *pikake* and bougainvillea. Most yards are cleared of rocks and cactus. Most water for daily use is obtained by catchment in 1,000-gallon wooden or concrete storage tanks.

All of the people on Niihau today speak English, but since Hawaiian is their first language, they often prefer to speak the language of their forefathers. There are no Hawaiian textbooks, so children learn Hawaiian by studying the Bible and singing Hawaiian church hymns at home. By studying the Bible, they learn the *loina*—the symbolic phrasing and poetry of the Hawaiian language. A favorite pastime of the children is trying to stump each other by reciting phrases from the Bible. The others must try to guess not only the chapter, but the verse. The months of the year on Niihau, as they are said in Hawaiian, reflect the differences between this Hawaiian island and all others:

Ikuwa	January	*Welo*	July
Welehu	February	*Ikiiki*	August
Makalii	March	*Kaaona*	September
Kaelo	April	*Hinaiaeleele*	October
Kaulua	May	*Hilina*	November
Nana	June	*Hilinehu*	December

In the middle of the town stands the only church on Niihau. It sits majestically among large, old *kiawe* trees and is surrounded by a stone wall covered with night-blooming cereus, with a quaint cemetery on the church grounds. The schoolhouse is within the churchyard. The influence of Christianity on Niihau lifestyle has been pervasive for the last one hundred years. In the nineteenth century, Francis Sinclair decreed that everyone on Niihau would go to church—even visitors. He went so far as to keep meticulous track of those who did not attend church and then punished them!

Sundays on Niihau are truly reserved for the Lord and observed as a day of rest. Early in the morning the church bells toll the hour at Iubile Church, and the rest of the island is quiet. During the service, some of the most beautiful choral singing in the Hawaiian chain can be heard. The voices are for the most part untrained, but their harmony and unrestrained quality are reminiscent of choral music heard throughout the South Pacific. The unique hymns heard on Niihau, however, are known only to the islanders. Their hymnal, *Buke Himeni Hawaii,* can be purchased only on Niihau, and there is no music notation, only lyrics. Melodies of familiar church hymns are used, with the islanders' own words.

Fishing, games and many other daily activities stop on the Sabbath. On Sunday evenings, the entire island listens to the "Gentle Moke" radio program from Kauai, which features Hawaiian music, talks, messages to Niihauans from off-island and a half hour of religious music.

A typical weekday on Niihau begins at five in the morning. The entire family participates in the morning *ohana* prayer service before the father leaves for work. Breakfast usually consists of the famous "Hawaiian pancakes" made from flour, water and sugar, or coffee and Saloon Pilot crackers and leftovers from the night before. Being a patriarchal family, much attention is given to the needs of the husband or father.

The Niihau man, usually dressed in jeans and boots, enjoys his work—even if it takes from dawn to midnight. A work day is not measured by an eight-hour day, but rather until a task is done. Boys begin working at fifteen or sixteen years of age. On an average, men work three days a week, mostly as paid cowboys for the Robinson ranch. The rest of their time is spent in gardening, fishing and similar work. If there is no work on Niihau, the men, sometimes with their families, can go to the Robinsons' business operations on Kauai. On Kauai, the workers live in camp-like areas called Pakala, Kapalawai, Kaawanui and Kekupua.

The men of Niihau make the most-desired charcoal in the state, so much so that supplies fall behind demand. Cutting down the *kiawe* trees, the men split them into short logs. The logs are put into large tile ovens, where they burn to coals and remain until cool, a process of several days. Once cool, the charcoal is broken into chunks and bagged for commercial use. The smaller chips are also gathered, bagged and sold for gardening purposes.

The women of Niihau attend to all of the usual household chores while raising the children in the old Hawaiian way. Children are obedient, and when not in school, they attend to their own chores as well as helping with the cooking and cleaning. As soon as children are able, they are given small duties and responsibilities. Great respect is shown by the younger generation for their parents and elders. When there are guests, the children sit to the side, often helping to serve the visitor. They are silent until spoken to, as was the old way. Usually the head of the house and the guest are served first, with the women and children eating later. Although the housewife has a kerosene stove in her kitchen, at times such as *luau* and parties, much of the cooking is often done in the traditional style—outside in the *imu*. The family often enjoys *kalua* pigs, sweet potatoes and other Hawaiian foods. Considerable flour is brought to the island, along with a few other food and grocery staples such as *poi*, salmon, Saloon Pilot crackers, taro, rice and soap. Few green vegetables are available on Niihau, so the housewife must order them from the store a week in advance.

At certain times of the year, the women will take the younger children to the beach for the day to search for the prized *pupu o Niihau*, the famous Niihau shells. Off-season, women spend a good deal of the day sorting and piercing shells, and making shell leis to sell. The additional income helps supplement the family budget. The majority of Niihau women dress in the traditional *muumuu*, although some women wear pants. There is no "women's movement" on Niihau—women serve to please their husbands and appear happy and content with their roles. When their husbands return home in the evenings after work, the women and children are there to greet them.

At the end of the typical day, the Niihau family is once again together. Making their own entertainment, the guitars and ukeleles are tuned and the songs begin. Before retiring for the night, the *ohana* prayers are repeated.

There are no airports, taxis, liquor, hotels, jails, post offices, cars, highways, bridges, harbors, shopping centers, tall buildings, theaters, beauty parlors or mongoose on Niihau. All mail to the residents of Niihau is sent to Makaweli, Kauai. There is, however, electricity, and politics. Niihauans are conscientious voters with 166 residents registered to vote in the one voting precinct. Traditionally a conservative Republican district, Niihauans voted Democratic in 1982 for the first time in their history.

Other signs of the outside modern world are becoming apparent. When Niihauans visit Kauai to see *ohana*, or to market their exquisite shell leis, they get a taste of change. Through their ingenuity, the men of Niihau have found other ways to tap into the "luxury" of things electric. They go off-island to seek motors from old lawn mowers. These are connected to alternators for electric lights. Solar energy lights some homes. Televisions are also powered by the home-made generators. Stereo radios and tape recorders connect families to the music and news from other islands. Some homes even contain such modern conveniences as sliding glass doors, louvered windows, wall paneling and carpeting. There are also five trucks on the island used for ranch work. Some of the inhabitants smoke tobacco, although the Robinson family has always tried to discourage the habit. Niihau is arid, and a serious fire could mean the destruction of the island—plus no one wants to see cigarette stubs littering the land.

Settled into their island home with these few changes, Niihauans are healthy and happy. They are rarely motivated to gain more material possessions beyond their basic needs. They have no worries about paying the mortgage on time; their homes are provided by the Robinson family, in keeping with an agreement with Kamehameha V at the time of the sale of the island to the family.

It is little surprise, then, that the Niihauans' most outstanding trait is friendliness with a smile and a handshake, a heritage they can be justly proud of. Though they may seem shy to outsiders, the islanders truly understand and express the *aloha* spirit and the *ohana* tradition, living and caring for one another. To a Niihauan, the entire island is *ohana*, and their usual greeting is the traditional Hawaiian sniffing kiss, touching nose to nose. Indeed, as one walks along the road passing their homes, voices call out from the dwellings, "*Hele mai ai.*" It is a greeting to share the bounty that is the blessing of the land, the family and the spirit.

CHAPTER II

The Sacred Days of Old on Niihau

He aloha Kaeo lei naulu
ke kuvini kaulana a Kahelelani

Beloved is Kaeo caressed by the naulu,
The famous wind of Kahelelani

Aerial of Kaunuapua Heiau and Keawanoi Bay. (*Photo: Bishop Museum*)

The Sacred Days of Old on Niihau

*T*HE ANCIENT HERITAGE of Niihau begins with a story of Pele—the fire goddess from Tahiti—that has been handed down from one island generation to the next since the beginning. Pele left Bora Bora and journeyed to the Hawaiian Islands, stopping first at Nihoa and then Niihau. While there, she tried to dig her fire pits, only to hit water. After her unsuccessful digging on Niihau, she left for Puukapele, Kauai, which also proved unsuitable, and so on down the Hawaiian chain to the island of Hawaii.

The place where Pele tried to dig her fire pits on Niihau is called Kaluakawila (very close to Kie Kie). The pit she dug extends from Kaluakawila to Puulama. This is a *malua*, or hole in the ground, but it is an elongated one that stretches all the way to Puulama. The *kupuna*, or elders, have a saying: "The first place that Pele set foot on in the Hawaiian chain was Niihau. Her foot is here on Niihau, but her body is in Hawaii, in the pits of Kilauea."

It is said that while Pele was with her lover Lohiau on Kauai, they made frequent trips to Niihau. Lohiau visited the island many times to surf. There is a chant in which there is much *kaona*, or double meaning, that Lohiau would say while playing the game of *kilu*. In this chant, Lohiau likens Pele to Kaula and Lohiau to Niihau:

Ke lei mai la Taula i te tai e	Kaula enwreathed by the ocean
ka malamalama o Niihau i ka malie	Niihau looms clear in the calm
a malama ke kaao o tou aloha	And clear is the tide of your love
tou aloha hoi ee.	The wonderful tide of your love.

There is a place on Niihau, called Motupapa, where Pele stood overlooking Kauai hoping she could find a home there. There are other references to the family of Pele in the place names of Paepaeohiiaka, Poliolehua, Kealahula and Makaohina.

Tahiti

Pele made the voyage from Tahiti in the south to Motu Papapa, Nihoa and to Niihau. All the gods who journeyed from Tahiti came first to Niihau before going on to the rest of the islands. This relates Niihauans to the high-ranking *alii*, or chiefs, who landed on Niihau and later left for Maui and

Kauai. Below is but one of the ancient chants from Niihau about the islands of Tahiti and of the travels between Niihau and Tahiti. This one speaks of visitors coming to Niihau from the south.

Ea mai ana ke ao ua o kona	The rain cloud of the south comes,
Ea mai ana ma Nihoa	It comes from Nihoa
Ma ta mole mai o Lehua	From beyond Lehua
Ua iho a pulu ke kahatai.	The rain has flooded the beach.

Composed by Kawelomahunalii

The people of Niihau remain firm in their belief of ties with the Tahitian people. The lower half of Niihau is teeming with legends, artifacts and petroglyphs relating to Tahiti and the Marquesas Islands. The *kupuna* made many ocean voyages back and forth to Tahiti using only the stars, winds, currents, birds and landmarks. Kapahee was the last to sail south, but his talent was passed on to his sons. Navigation was done during the months of the trades, both going and returning. Nihoans and Niihauans were of the highest royal blood lines from a long-forgotten but very sacred island, and as such they kept to themselves, except for visits to Kauai.

Heiau ✦ Temples

The religion of Niihau before the introduction of Christianity reflects a strong memory of the ancient homeland. Most of the *heiau* or temples that remain on the island face toward the west or Tahiti, following old migration patterns from Niihau to Nihoa, Motu Papapa and Tahiti, and then back again. The people of old expressed their religious sentiments through the spiritual union of the past, the land, ocean, sky, man and the gods. The number of ancient temples that remain on Niihau are numerous and can still be found at the following locations:

Kaunupou heiau is a koa, or fishing shrine, located at Kaunupou.

Pueo heiau at Puu Pueo, where several other temples are located.

Kahalekuamano heiau at Nanina, which is about 1,000 feet east of Kalanihale Point. The temple is a low embankment, thirty-five feet long and five feet wide.

Kaunuokaha (Kaunuohiki) heiau is located south of Lehua landing, on shore about one mile northeast of Kaunuapua. This *heiau* is a small, low platform.

Kaunuapua heiau is a *puuhonua* or place of refuge located next to Puu Koae at Kihawahine. It is an oblong enclosure built of limestone slabs with a low bench encircling the exterior walls. The bench on the outside and the entrance facing inland (east) are unusual features. In many places, the base of the walls are faced with large slabs set on edge. There were interior enclosures at each end for the altars.

Pahau heiau is on the eastern shore of Kawaihoa. In addition to the temple, there are remnants of an old village found at this site with *paepae* or stone foundations. In 1867, *The Pacific Commercial Advertiser* made reference to a leper settlement near this area.

Puhi Ula heiau was reported in 1912 by John Stokes to be at Puhi Ula, although the remains cannot be seen.

Kauwaha heiau is hidden by nature and buried under the sands at Kaununui. The temple exposes itself only under certain circumstances. This unveiling takes place when there is a tidal wave or extremely rough waters. Kauwaha is a very large *heiau*. Its upright walls are made of black rock. Among those Niihauans fortunate enough to have seen this *heiau* during the 1946 tidal wave were Tutu Kaui and Olivia Kamala. There is a special saying for Kaununui that also includes the name of the *heiau*: "*Kaununui heiau kapu noho ana i ka poli o Kauwaha*," meaning "the sacred temple Kauwaha is cradled in the bosom of Kaununui."

The *alii* or chiefs who ruled in the days of *heiau* are still remembered on Niihau for their greatness of leadership and astounding physical attributes. Kahelelani was the first of the great chiefs who ruled some ten generations ago. His name is now recalled as the name of the true *pupu*, or shell, of Niihau. Another great *alii* was Kaoahi, or "fire thrower." This queen of Niihau is talked about in the Pele legend. Halulu and Halalii were also great chiefs of Niihau. Halulu had a thunderous voice; Halalii was a wandering soul. Niihau's lakes were named after these chiefs. Kamaakamikioi and Kamaakauluohia were sons of Halulu who were skilled runners without equal in all the Hawaiian Islands. It is said that they could run on land or sea, earth or sky. One of the kings of Niihau was Puwalu, who ruled during the time Manokalanipo was ruling Kauai.

Kaeo

The great *alii* who was successful in the unification of Niihau was Kaeo. Ruler of the northern portion of Niihau, he was very much loved and admired by the people of his island. However, there was another warlike chief on Niihau named Kawaihoa who was greedy and wanted Kaeo's portion of land. Much strife took place between the two *alii*, and in order to mark off their boundary, a stone wall—Papohaku—was built across the southern quarter of the island. Kaeo's identifying markers were represented by black stones and Kawaihoa's by white stones.

Kaeo eventually united the entire island under his rule with the help of his two brothers from Maui. One brother was Kaiana, the other his half-brother, Kahekili, King of Maui. It is said that these brothers often joined and went to war together. When they came to Niihau, they landed on the sandy shore of Kamakaua. The two Maui brothers were so strong that it is said of them, *"Elua no mapuna hoe, kau i ka aina"* — "Two strokes of the paddle to reach land." King Kaeo was such a gentle man that he did not wish to spill the blood of his people, so he let his two brothers do the fighting. One of the brothers was not a fast runner but was very strong. One time he threw his spear through fifty men as they were running away. The other brother would chase down his enemy for the kill. After the bloodshed, the battleground was called Pali Kamakaua, *pali* being the heaps of dead bodies. On Kawaihoa's side of the island, all white stones can be seen, while up on Kaeo's boundary white stones are mixed with black stones. Because King Kaeo was so loved by the people, he was taken to the middle of the island, while Kawaihoa was banished to the southern end of the island.

Genealogical charts show that Kaeo (Kaeokulani) married a high-born woman called Kamakahelei and to this union a future king, Kaumualii, was born in 1790. It is said that Kauai and Niihau carried the highest blood lines in the Hawaiian chain. Some former rulers are:

Puwalu	Kahelelani
Manoopupaipai (queen)	Kaoahi (queen)
Makalii	Halalii
Kaneoneo	Kupoloula
Kaeo	

Lua Kupapau ✦ Burials

On Niihau's lofty cliffs are numerous royal burial caves where the sacred bones of the *alii* are concealed. The largest is said to be the ancestral cave of Manokalanipo. Julius Rodman wrote of his 1934 experience entering several Niihau burial caves in his work, *Kahuna Sorcerers*. He learned of the cave from two Niihau men—Maui Kaiwi, then a newspaper boy at Fort and King streets in Honolulu, and Kimo, who was living on Kauai. These two men had lived on Niihau during the time of Aubry Robinson and were boyhood friends. Learning of these caves, Rodman convinced the men to take him with them on a visit.

Upon entering the first cave, they noted numerous skeletons piled on top of each other near the entrance. To the rear there were several different chambers. One chamber contained many mummified bodies of the *alii* rank.

All of these bodies lay in a row with the heads to the east and feet to the west. Each one was adorned completely with *palaoa*, or necklaces, and feather amulets. Each was covered with black tapa topped with *makaloa* mats. There was a layer of dust three inches thick in the cave, which must have taken more than a century to accumulate through the small cracks in the cave's opening (a small door through which the caretaker could enter). The explorers left the caves in unexpected haste, leaving the sacred site intact. Tutu Kaui verified the existence of these caves.

The people of old buried the common people along with human sacrifices in sand dunes. There are many burial caves, sand dunes, hills and ridges on Niihau, such as Nawahahunakele and Kapalikalahale. Near Nanina, there are deep underground caves close to Kahalekuamano Heiau.

Olelo ✦ Language

The remains of the people of old are not only found in the ancient temples, burial sites and legends of chiefs, but also in the historic *olelo*, or language, that survives on Niihau. Today, the Niihauans have preserved the purity of the Hawaiian language of their forefathers and on Niihau it is spoken in its purest form. As with the older language of the Hawaiians, the use of the "T" and "K" are interchanged. The "L" and "R" change, as do the "L" and "N." Although the language is written with the "K," Niihauans remain true to the ancestral tongue in speech with the use of the "T." As Captain James Cook noted during his visit to the islands in 1778, this style of language has almost the same sound as in Tahiti, though it is much softer and less brash and guttural in sound.

Prior to 1822, all the islands appeared to have used the interchange of the "T" and "K," although in songs, chants and poetic compositions the "T" was universally used. However, when the Christian missionaries developed a written language, they standardized the spelling by using the "K" instead of the "T" in written documents. Thus in the first hymn book, consisting of sixty songs, they went contrary to the verbal practice of the traditional Hawaiian by using the "K." Correct usage or not, the written form set the pattern for a new pronunciation. The isolation of Niihau has preserved it from language changes that occurred on other islands.

On Niihau it is believed that there were three different levels of the Hawaiian language: literal, figurative and esoteric. The most common usages were the literal and figurative. The esoteric was for only the highest and most-sacred persons. The *kaona*, or figurative language, was spoken in riddles to hide its true meaning; this was used also to stimulate the mind. Expressed in riddles, puns and hidden multiple meanings, the *kaona* attests to the high intellectual levels of abstract thought that Niihauans attained.

Olelo Nane ✦ Riddles

The language of the people of old was full of riddles. They talked and even lived in parables. This facility of expression led to constant playing of word games. For example, one of the special places on Niihau, reserved for *kamaaina*, is a small hill called Puu o Hawaii. As visitors would come to visit the island and go sightseeing, the *kamaaina* would ask of the visitors, "Have you seen all of Niihau?" When the visitor answered, "Yes," the *kamaaina* would then ask, "Have you seen Puu o Hawaii," and if the visitor said no, the *kamaaina* said, "Not only have you not seen Niihau, you have not seen the rest of the Hawaiian chain." There is a saying that relates to this area: *"Puka o Hawaii i Niihau"* — "The ancient gate to Hawaii is Niihau." This is an example of the word and mind games that went on daily. Testing and trying to catch the other person was the entertainment of the day.

Olelo Noeau ✦ Poetic Sayings

Riddles, boasts, taunts, bragging, word play and proverbs were commonly passed between the islands of Niihau and Kauai. Since there was much inter-island trade in the ancient days, it was a favorite pastime. Some of these fascinating sayings are:

Pae mahu o Kauwai nei — "Hermaphrodite of Kauai." *Mahu* also meant sexless or without. This is from a string figure chant.

Ekolu no pua lawa kuu lei — "The three flowers (children). My lei is complete."

Ekolu lakou keiki — "They are the three children." This and the previous saying pertain to ancient times. These were triplets born of Hina, the goddess of creation, on the same day. No other children were born. They were named Niihau, Kaula and Nihoa.

O kanaka o ka wai — "The people of the water." This was used in reference to Kauai.

Ke hoi nei ko Niihau keiki i ka maluhia ka ulu hala o Halawela — "When Niihau's children return, there will be peace in the *hala* grove of Halawela." This is a 1865 lament for the return of the island to the natives.

Aahu ae i ka pawehe o Niihau ai la oe i ka manu o Kaula — "The mats of Niihau you shall wear and the birds of Kaula you will eat." Niihau is alone number one for the *alii*.

Ai la oe i ka manu o Kaula — "You then rule the birds of Kaula." The ruling domain of hero Kawelo.

Ka ua lihau anu toetoe koou, ha ahi ka ke kapa o ka ua i lala ai — "When the rain comes it is bitter cold. The fire is your blanket that will do away with the rain."

I ka lani no ka ua wai e no ke pulu — "The rain is still in the clouds. It's time to prepare the mulch." Months in advance, Niihauans prepared the land for planting, usually for *uwala*. Don't wait for the rain to come; you may find yourself with little or no crop.

Pua ea ka manu o Kaula i ke kai — "The birds of Kaula die at sea." Do not wander too far from home lest you be destroyed.

Hanau Niihau he aina, he motu, he aina i ke aa i ka mole o ta aina — "Born the island of Niihau, the land that is the stem of all the islands." Niihau is oldest of the eight Hawaiian islands.

Au ka toae, he la malie — "When the koae swims, it is a calm day." It's a good fishing day.

Ma ka mole mai o Lehua — "By the foundation of Lehua." Lehua and Niihau are one, as they were one island before sinking.

Moku ka ili la — "Sun-snatching island," referring to Lehua.

Ena aku la manu o Kaula — "The birds of Kaula are wild," speaking of a shy person. From *Olelo Noeau,* by Mary Pukui.

Niihau o Manoopupaipai — Queen Manoopupaipai of Niihau, an ancient *alii*. A second meaning is "Niihau, island of belly-slapping," referring to the heavy population on Niihau. People made fun of the many births. In days of old, Niihau, Kauai and Maui were the most-heavily populated of all the Hawaiian islands.

He ku pu maia ike ala — "The banana stalk that stands by the road," referring to a person who was sexually impotent. The stalk was pithy and no good.

Kauai kaili la, o Niihau ka la kau — "Kauai steals the sun; Niihau is the sun."

Kaulana Nualolo i ka haka lewa ke ala kunihi a ka malihini — "Famous is the swinging ladder of Nualolo, a steep road for the newcomer."

Hoona ke ola i ka malu hau o Halalii — "Comfortable is the life in the shade of the tree at Halalii."

Hula ✦ Dance

The *hula* was a sacred way of communicating with religious significance that also contained important traditions and hidden meanings.

The following two stories about hula on Niihau are quoted from the book *Hula: Historical Perspectives,* by Dorothy B. Barrere, Mary K. Pukui and Marion Kelly. These dances were brought with the Niihau people when they migrated to the island of Kauai to inhabit the Nualolo and Kalalau valleys. Since Niihauans frequently sailed back and forth between Kauai, much of the Niihau culture has been assimilated into the Kauai culture.

Hula Kii

In 1899, Moses Manu described this dance in an article for the newspaper *Ka Loea Kalaiaina*. It has been translated by Mary Kawena Pukui in the book *Hula: Historical Perspectives*. The dance was first performed on Niihau by a sister of Pele, Kapoulakinau. Kapoulakinau started to chant and her younger sister, Kawelani, also known as Nawahineliilii, performed this dance that was never seen before. Kapo's voice rose like the gentle-eyed lale bird. Her hands were uplifted to gesture in her chanting.

Hiki mai, hiki mai ka la	It has come, it has come, the sun
Aloha wale ka la e kau nei	How I love the sun that is on high
Aia malalo o Kawaihoa	Below is Kawaihoa
A ka lalo o Kauai, o Lehua.	On the incline of Kauai is Lehua.

As the chant ended, Kawelani strutted like a bird onto the *moena* and rolled back the irises of her eyes until only the whites showed, as bright as the mother-of-pearl shell. This act made everyone shout with excitement. Thrilled with her comical stunt, they kept shouting and laughing. The dance that this maiden performed for Chief Halalii was the *Hula Kii*. The people of Niihau perpetuated the dance. As this dance was an interpretation of the wooden images, it was danced in a stiff manner, sometimes sticking out the stomachs and mimicking how the images looked.

Papa Hehi and Kalaau

Niihau was also known for the treadle-board dance. According to John Kaimikaua, there was an old chant taught to him by his hula instructor that tells of Laka's first *halau* on Niihau. In 900 A.D., Laka sailed from Molokai to Niihau, landing on the shores of Kauno (possibly Kaunu—the ancient name in priestly language). A plank in the canoe had come loose. She put her foot on the plank and while she was chanting, she kept time with her foot on the loose plank. Thus was created the heel-toe treadle-board dance.

The following chant was written for Kapiolani by the people of Niihau as she toured Kauai. It tells of the love for the island and all its beauty.

The Sacred Days of Old on Niihau II

E hoi ke aloha Niihau E	Our love goes out to you from Niihau,
i ka Wai-huna-o-ka-paoo	of the hidden waters of the *paoo*,
Na-ulu-hua-i-ka-hapapa E	The breadfruit on the reef
mehe ko eli lima o Halalii E	like the cane dug by hand of Halalii,
I ea Nihoa mahope E	Here is Nihoa behind
i ke lau hapapa ike kai E	the seaweed reef in the ocean
O ka la welawela ike kula E	The hot sun on the plains
huli aku ke alo i Kauai E	turn to face Kauai,
Haina ka inoa no ka Wahina E	This is the name of the lady,
no Kapiolani no, he inoa E	Kapiolani is the name.

Older hula included *Hula Kilelei* and *Hula Ipu Wai*. The following hula was written by Kalekahee. It tells of a trip he took with his friend.

Aloha Niihau ✦ Moena Pawehe Hula

Aia i Niihau kuu pawehe	Niihau is where my *pawehe* is,
he moena e pahee ai ko ili.	A mat that glides on the skin.
Hauna noeau a ka Mikioi.	The Mikioi skillful at stroking,
kamakani no welo piko o Lehua.	The wind that seeks the center of Lehua.
Elua maua me kuu aloha	There are two of us,
na ulu hua i ka hapapa.	And my love that lives in the reef.
Kau aku ka mano ae ike maka	A memory returned of something I have seen with my eyes,
na ko eli lima a o Halalii.	The cane dug by hand at Halalii.
Ailana o Kaula i ka mole olu	The island of Kaula
home pohai mau a na manu.	Is the ancestral home of the birds.
He aloha Nihoa i ka ehu kai	Beloved is Nihoa in the salt spray,
a ka naulu ae hooipo nei.	Courted by the naulu winds.
O oe kuuipo alo o ke anu	You are my elusive cool sweetheart
na ale holu mai o Kaulakahi.	The rippling swells from Kaulakahi.
Hookahi au lei ae lei nei	One lei do I have on,
o kahi wai kau mai ao Kamaile.	That waterfall from Kamaile.
E ake manao ae ike aku	A thought occurred to me that
keahi kau mai ao Aneki	I wish to see the high fire from Aneki.
Ka nihi no welo i Makuaiki	The rim of the cliffs at Makuaiki,
he ike kou aloha eha nei kino.	Your love is little and it hurts my body.
Kaulana Nualolo i ka haka lewa	Famous is the swinging ladder of Nualolo,
ke ala kunihi a ka malihini.	A steep road for the newcomer.
Iini kamanao ae ike maka	Strong is my desire to see with my eyes,
kahi wai kaulana o Waialoha.	The famous waters of Waialoha.

He aloha ae an ike koolau *kamakani noho lae o Kikipua.*	You have this love for the Koolau, The wind that lives at the point of Kikiopua.
Kuupua he lehua ai Haena *kaena i ka wai a o Limahuli*	My lehua blossom is at Haena, At Haena also are the waters of Limahuli.
Ka huli ke ala o ka nae'nae *kuu ipo lauae noho i Makana.*	The fragrance of the *naenae* the sweetheart shrub That grows on Makana.
Kaua ike one o Maniniholo *kuuipo ike kai holu o Makua.*	You and I at the sand of Maniniholo, Reveals the rippling of the sea at Makua.
Ulu hala o Naue kau aloha *i ka nou hala ole a ka lupua.*	The *hala* groves of Naue I love, Exposed to the hurtling lupua wind.
Healoha na lehua o Luuluupali *noho ana i ka poli o ka au maka*	Beloved is the lehua of Luuluupali, Cradled in the bosom of Aumaka.
Hiki aku ike one a o Hoohila *hue pau e ke kai a o Kealahula.*	I reached the sands of Hoohila, This is the end of the sea of Kealahula.
Kau aku kamanao no Hanalei *e ike i ka nani o Kaualoku.*	Thoughts come to me of Hanalei, To see the beauty of Kaualoku.
Haina ia mai hana kapuana *moena pawehe ai ko ili.*	This tells my story of The mat that glides on the skin.

Written by Kalekahee

Although there is no formal hula instruction on Niihau today, the dance is still performed at parties and celebrations.

Kapua ✦ Demigods

The *olelo* and hula of the people not only contain *kaona*, but also the *kaao* or legendary stories and mysteries that are passed between the generations. Tales are still told of *kupua*, or demigods, like the one who came from Kauai (spelled Kauwai in the old way) long ago and was so powerful he could split large boulders through concentration accompanied by chanting. There were also *makaula* or prophets among the people of old, great seers such as Hulumaniani who also visited Niihau from Kauai.

Moo

One of the beings of old was the *moo*, or supernatural lizard, that inhabited the waters of Niihau. One large *moo* was Lehuakona, who came to Niihau from Tahiti. Lehu was another large *moo* who came from Tahiti with his two sister *moo*. After such a long trip, the girls were tired. As they neared Niihau, the sisters wished to rest, but Lehu spotted the island of Kauai and told the girls they could stay if they wished, but that Kauai was more lush in vegetation. The sisters remained on Niihau, while Lehu went on to Kauai. Lehu went ashore at Lawai, where he rested from the long trip. Upon waking, Lehu looked around this new place until he spotted an underground tunnel. Lehu decided to investigate this underwater tunnel, but because he was so large, he got stuck inside where he now lives today. His crying can be heard at the Spouting Horn on Kauai. He still cries for help from his sisters who remained on Niihau.

Mano

There were two major *mano,* or sharks, who made their home in the waters around Niihau. Kuhaimoana, a shark god who lived in the cave at Kaula, was said to be the brother of Pele. Being a *kupua,* he was able to assume other forms. Kuhaimoana was reported to be of a very large species, migrating to Niihau with Pele from Tahiti. This great sacred shark was an *aumakua,* an ancestral guardian, to the people. Sometime in the past, a pact was made with him to protect the people and the surrounding waters from intruders.

Offerings of many varieties were given to Kuhaimoana. The offering might have been only a red handkerchief, but Niihauans always paid their respects to this deity. Kuhaimoana would not allow anyone go to Kaula to molest the birds, because they led the fishermen to the schools of fish. Part of the agreement with the Niihau people was that the sharks would not eat the fish that the people enjoyed.

Kukaiaiki was the shark of Lehua *motu* and of the Kaulakahi Channel between Kauai and Niihau. His cave was located on the west side of Lehua; he was Kuhaimoana's son. Although sharks abound in the waters of Niihau, the people are not afraid of them. Islanders swim in the water with the sharks nearby. Even though many tales have been told of men swimming in shark-infested waters, no shark attacks have been recorded on Niihau. Other *aumakua,* or guardians, include the *pueo,* the owl, and *honu,* or turtle.

Huna Motu

One of the most persistent mysteries of Niihau to this day is the legend of the *huna motu*—the mysterious islands that have been occasionally sighted by islanders and outsiders. In fact, the first recorded sighting of these "disappearing islands" was by Captain James Cook in 1778, who wrote that he could see Oahu to the east and over to the southwest another island, small and uninhabited. He called these islands Moodoopapapa. He returned to the seas of Niihau twice to find the elusive and mysterious turtle islands but was never successful in sighting them again.

The Niihau people of old knew of these islands, as they were used as points of reference during the many travels back and forth to Tahiti. They are included in many chants and legends and have been documented in historic times by others in addition to Cook. In his study of the geology of Niihau, scientist Norman Hinds reported that three miles northwest of Kaula was a rocky pinnacle that stood thirty-eight feet above the ocean surface. Niihauan Keola Kauileilehua Keamoai was eyewitness to a floating island. Perhaps the islands are what Hawaiian mythologist Martha Beckwith speaks of as the twelve sacred islands of Kane.

One of these *huna motu* is known as Unulani. There is a marker on Kawaihoa, the southern volcano, where people who wished to see the island of Unulani would go. They would stay there all night, not to miss the island that can be seen only before sunrise—the island disappears after the sun has risen. As soon as the Unulau wind blows, many head for the mountain, hoping to see this beautiful island that is lush with fruit, animals and houses. Tutu Kaui was one of the fortunate persons to witness this island. M. W. K. Keale prophesized, "The island will disappear and not be seen again until the last generation."

Kahikipapaialewa, Kanehunamotu and Kuaihelani are three other islands that float in the ocean and appear just before the break of dawn on the eastern side of Niihau. They were always seen on *kapu* days. They were very lush—trees laden with fruits, the surrounding ocean full of fish, and everything plentiful. It is said that only the spiritual believers can see these islands. It is also believed that they are the path to Kahiki, land of the gods. If the gods permit the islands to move close, then it will only take an hour to reach them. If the gods don't see fit to let them to get close, one could sail the ocean and never find them. They are seen at sunrise and sunset.

In this sacred world of worship, spirit, and legend, *ka poe kahiko o Niihau*—the people of old—pursued for a thousand years their daily customs, manners and lifestyles, striving to maintain the harmony of their gods, the earth, the sea and the sky.

CHAPTER III

Ka Poe Kahiko —
The People of Old

*He keiki mai au no na kiu eiwa
he kiu kamakani anu o Niihau*

I am a child from the lands of the
nine *kiu* winds, the cold winds of Niihau

Alice Kahuanui Niheu-Kaina demonstrates *hei*. *(Photo: Bishop Museum)*

KA POE KAHIKO, or ancient ones, lived from the bounty of the ocean and the land. Their skills at fishing and *mahiai,* or agriculture, were nurtured for a thousand years through close association with nature. The ingenuity of Niihauans in early times is seen in their farming methods. They irrigated their land through the use of the *ohe kahiki,* or bamboo, to carry water from the *punawai,* or springs, lakes and ponds down to the area of planting.

They knew that the *lepo,* or dirt, on the dry slopes was good for the sweet potato, and that *uwala,* or sweet potato, planting should begin just as rainy season starts. They kept it growing during the dry season by planting on the protected southeast side of the island.

The Niihauans were skilled at growing food on *kula,* or dry, land. They had small taro patches at Waiu on the windward side. To conserve moisture, they mulched for months before they planted. They prepared the mounds of loose dirt for long periods before they planted the sweet potato, usually just before the rainy months arrived. They planted two or three slips into each hole, and as the vines grew, they would twist them around the mound. During growing stages, they continued to keep the dirt loose. They would pick the largest potatoes as soon as they were ready so the others could receive more energy from the earth.

The Niihauans also built terraces for planting. They were hard workers: cultivation of *kula* lands is a long, trying task. Niihau produced more sugar cane, bananas, sweet potatoes, yams and salt than did Kauai. They understood the cycles of the year that were most productive for planting certain crops and when inactivity was proper. As one saying goes, *"Welehu i ka mahina hoomakaukau ka uluna,"* which means "February is the month to make ready the pillow." In other words, in February there is little work to be done.

Uwala ✦ Sweet Potato

The knowledge of agriculture was of course specialized to each crop that the native people of old cultivated. The *uwala,* the sweet potato, had many varieties. Some of the names for the sweet potato on Niihau in days of old included:

wailua	palani	huamoa
manamana	malihini	halamomona
kalia	uwala-kahiki	eleelemahina
kamalino	heuhi	mohihi
naniekolu	piku	kalo
eleele	o ka ipu momona	kepu
paha	huapala	

Today, as the rainy season starts on Niihau, there is a mad scramble by everyone to get sweet potato slips so they can begin planting. Almost every household grows sweet potato, and when the rainy season rolls around, planting is the most important thing to do. Gourds are intercropped with the *uwala*. Three to four months later, it is time to kill a pig because the potatoes are ready. *Kalua* pig and sweet potatoes are a tradition. The leaves of the *uwala* are sometimes eaten as well. There were over 100 acres of *uwala* planted at Kamalino. A wonderful *poi* was made of sweet potatoes, as reflected in the song "Aloha Ka Manini."

Since the whole island helps in the planting and preparations, if someone was missing without good reason and then at harvest time wanted his share, this saying was heard:

Ua ka ua i Taeo, ihea oe	When it rained on Kaeo, where were you?
I Niihau no mawaho?	On Niihau?
Ua ka ua i Taeo, ihea oe	When it rained on Kaeo, where were you?
I Kauai i no maloko mai?	On Kauai?

This meant if you didn't help, why should you now want to share in the harvest? No work, no food. This kind of person is considered stingy and lazy.

Ulu ✦ Breadfruit

Unlike other islands in Hawaii, there were only five breadfruit trees or *elima kumu ulu pau loa* on Niihau. Each of these trees had an individual name: *Hikinaakala, Kulimoku, Hakaleleaponi, Kalama* and *Nauluhuaikahapapa*. These five trees once grew in the Kawaihoa area. The only one that remains is *Nauluhuaikahapapa*. This tree was planted close to the beach in a limestone reef. In this reef are large holes up to ten feet deep. The tree was planted in the hole so that the roots could reach water, otherwise it could not get water on the reef—a brilliant bit of planting. As the tree grew up toward the sun, the leaves and fruit were at reef level, thus the name, *Nauluhuaikahapapa*. There are many more holes in the reef where the last surviving *ulu* tree grows. In them are planted ti plants and mango trees. The mangos are also picked at reef level. The people have not further propagated the *ulu* tree, as they no longer use the breadfruit as a staple.

Uhi ✦ Yams

Na kiwi a holei was a giant, ancient yam plant that grew near Kawaihoa, close to the five *ulu* trees. Individual tubers over three feet long were reported. Its bark was very rough from the dirt line to the narrowed middle, while the upper part of the plant was smooth-skinned. The leaves looked like the *pohuehue*, or morning glory. Sometimes, when there were no slips of *uwala* to plant, people planted slips of this *uhi*.

This *uhi* is called *kupala*. One of its most unusual characteristics is its root system. The main roots appear like two large legs, and from these grow several smaller roots which, at the ends, have the potato. This giant *uhi* tastes like an Irish potato and is white inside. The whaling ships that put into port at Niihau stocked their ships with these yams, preferred by the ships' captains as they kept longer than the sweet potato or taro. The ships also took a supply of *uwala*.

The Niihauans baked these giant *uhi* in an *imu*, or oven (the word *umu*, an older spoken version of *imu*, was in use on Niihau as late as the mid-1800s). The *uhi* was eaten in the old days during famine. It was also used for medicinal purposes. Tutu Kaui said that he remembered that some of them were so large and heavy that a horse could only carry two at a time.

Paakai ✦ Salt

The people of old were also adept at manufacturing *paakai*, or salt. This was a natural sea salt created by evaporation. At Lake Halulu and on the southern coast at Leahi, salt was collected. The finest and whitest salt—almost powder-fine—was from Niihau. The pure white color was obtained by scraping off the salt from the top of the foam, where no dirt mixed in with the salt. Niihauans did not have salt pans as on Kauai. As intermittent lakes would evaporate, pure salt would remain. There were several grades of Niihau salt. Occasionally they would directly mix in the *alaea*, or clay, as some medicines required *alaea*. This mixture is a brownish-red color.

Makani ✦ Winds

Understanding the produce of the land and sea also required understanding *kamakani o Niihau*, or the winds of Niihau. The types of wind that blew across their island were each identified and named by the people of old. These winds included:

> **Kona**, a strong, sometimes violent wind from the southwest, accompanied by the rains. This wind is also known as the Konaelua, as it has two distinct natures.

Konahea, a cold south wind from Kaula.

Konalani, a lighter southern wind.

Naulu, a fair, gentle wind from the north, sometimes known as "royal wind." The canoes traveled from Niihau to Kauai during this time.

Moae, a northeast trade wind.

Mikioi, the strong, gusty wind from Lehua, usually an afternoon wind.

Koolau, an angry wind bringing choppy waters.

Kiu, very cold wind that lingers on Niihau.

Kiu-Koolau, a moderately cold northwestern wind.

Kiu-Kalalau, very cold and high wind from Kalalau on Kauai. The ocean becomes choppy.

Kiu-Mana, a cold wind that blows from Mana, Kauai.

Kiu-Puukapele, also a wind from Kauai at Puukapele.

Kiu-Lokuloku, gale winds.

Kiu-Lehua, a very cold wind from the northeast. Due to its mixture of Lehua and Kiu winds, the coldness is intensified.

Kiu-Pekekeu, a light, feathering cold wind.

Kiu-Peapea, a cross wind that brings evil, war and other troubles.

Kiu-Kulepe, an ocean wind that overturns canoes.

Aoa, a very strong wind from Hanapepe, Kauai, well-liked by the people of Niihau. This wind affords good travel between the islands.

Aoalaenihi, a northeast wind that brings rain. It is also known as the *alii* wind, as it comes very quietly on Niihau.

Lehua, a wind that comes to Niihau from Lehua. Like the Naulu wind, the Lehua is a northeastern trade, but it stirs up a bit more.

Inuwai, a sea breeze, a water-absorbing wind.

Unulau, a northeast trade wind that brings rain to Niihau. Also associated with the appearance of the floating island Unulani.

Wiliahiu, a wild, untamed whirlwind at possible hurricane velocity.

Papaainuwai, a gentle wind that the people of Kauai sail to Niihau. Sometimes it is accompanied by a misty rain; other times it is with the sun (also called Paa a la).

Puaia, a slight breeze off the ocean causing ripples in the water.

Aeloa, a strong trade wind from Kauai.

Leialoha, a caressing wind.

Laaakaa, definition unknown.

The many names used by the ancients to describe the winds were often named for the area from where they came. Many brought warnings, each was a prophecy of things to come. The old Niihauans were acutely aware of the most minute changes in the weather. This was necessary, as weather governed their entire existence. Temperature differentials are noticeable between Niihau and Kauai. Open exposure to the cold north winds cause lower temperatures on Niihau than at similar elevations on Kauai.

As was common for the people of old, their knowledge frequently was expressed in their poetic chants, or *mele*, and sayings. The following separate sayings reflected the influences of winds on their lives.

He keiki mai au no na kiu eiwa, he kiu kamakani anu o Niihau — "I am a child from the lands of the nine *kiu* winds, the cold winds of Niihau."

He Lehua kamakani olu o Niihau. He Leialoha kamakani pumehana oka aina o Niihau — "The Lehua wind caresses Niihau. The Leialoha is the most cherished and dearest wind of Niihau."

O Niihau no eka oi apuni mai Hawaii moku o Keawe, O Kauwai moku o Manokalanipo loku ia e ka ua Naulu — "Niihau is the best of all from Hawaii, island of Keawe, to Kauai of Manokalanipo drenched in the downpour of the Naulu."

Hooulu ia e ke Konalani i ka no ke hala ole aka Naulu, a ke ahe Lehua me ka Mikioi o ka Inuwai me ka Moae — "The Konalani makes everything grow with the persistence of the Naulu. The breath of Lehua, the Mikioi, the Inuwai, and the Moae."

Kahiko eka nani oka aina o ke Konahea pile me oe — "Beautiful is the land from the days of old with the Konahea wind caressing you."

Waiaka hani i ka makani na kiu eiwa koni ika ili — "Waiaka flirts with the winds, the nine cold winds that tingle the skin."

Heaha la ia mea i ke keiki Unulau o Hina? Ke hooua mai, he ola pai Niihau — "What is this to the Unulau child of Hina? When it rains, life touches Niihau."

Ka malamalama o Niihau ua malie, malie hakakau ko aloha e ka Inuwai — "Niihau shines in the calm, peaceful with the Inuwai that embraces her with love."

O oe ka ia eka Inuwai e hooipo nei me Leahi — "You are the main course Inuwai courting Leahi."

Hanohano Niihau i kau ike, aka Naulu ae hooipo nei — "Famous is the Niihau I see, caressed and loved by the Naulu wind."

Mele of the Winds on Niihau

Hanohano Niihau i kau ike aka Naulu ae hooipo nei	Famous is the Niihau I see caressed and loved by the Naulu.
He makani kaulana no ka aina kolonahe mai ana i ka paeopua	Celebrated wind of the island blowing softly to the horizon.
He pua lei oe na kealoha ahe milimili hoi naka puuwai	A child of love my lei, a favorite of my heart.
Heaha nei hana a ka Unulau kamakani i kekaha o Halalii?	What are you up to Unulau, parading back and forth at Halalii?
He alii e ka manu kau mai iluna mena ulu hua ae kaulana nei	Above soars the bird like an alii and the famous ulu fruit.
E hoi e pili meka Moae kamakani ika luna o Kawaihoa	Come and be together with the Moae, the wind that blows on Kawaihoa.
O oe ka-ia e ka Inuwai e hooipo nei me Leahi	You are the main course Inuwai courting Leahi.
Kahiko e ka nani o ka aina o ke Konahea pili me oe	Beautiful is the land from the days of old with the Konahea caressing you.
Eia mai au a hiki aku o ke Konalani poina ole	Wait for me, I'm coming, the unforgettable Konalani.
Aole hoi au kamakani Kona o ke ahe mai au a ke Koolau	I am not the Kona wind but the softly blowing Koolau.
Aia kaiini la-i Lehua aka Mikioi ae hii-mai nei	The desire is at Lehua cradled in the arms of the Mikioi.
Helehuakamakani kau aheahe hooheno i ka luna o Kaaliwai	Softly and gently is the Lehua caressing the heights of Kaaliwai.
Ua lawa keia meke aloha ua kokua mai ka makualani	My song is ending with love and guidance from heaven above.
E ola kakou a mau loa akau i ke ao malamalama	May we live long until we ride the clouds of heaven.
Haina ia mai ana kapuana hanohano Niihau i kau ike.	So ends my story, famous is the Niihau I have seen.

Na Mea Hana Kahiko O Ke Au ✦ Artifacts

The intimacy that the people of old felt for nature was also reflected in their daily arts, tools and crafts. Archaeological treasures of inestimable value reflecting this heritage still remain undisturbed on Niihau. The island's isolation means that many ancient sites have been untouched by scientists or vandals. Due to the extensive exports and trade on Niihau before the island's purchase in 1864, there are some Niihau artifacts in museums and private collections.

All over the island, the artifacts of the ancient ones lay both under and on top of the sand. They include large stones that were used as sharpening tools for the spear makers. They sharpened the spear by holding it upright between two hands and twirling it at a fast speed, leaving indentations in the stone.

Ancient *palaoa*, or royal necklaces, made of mother-of-pearl shell in the "*lei opuu*" design are found. The chain hole is star-shaped, showing its antiquity. Many pearl fishhooks are being destroyed by breakage. These artifacts are very important to the study of the Polynesian peoples.

Na Mea Hana ✦ Tools

The ancient tools, or *na mea hana*, used on Niihau were crafted from natural materials. The adzes were made of a blackish or red-colored stone. Knives were usually made of shell, bamboo, shark's teeth or a combination of materials. For drilling, a pointed stick, shell or bone was used. By twirling a drill at a fast speed, craftsmen could make holes used to connect two objects. Stones were used to make holes as well as for pounding. For planting and digging holes, or just to simply loosen the dirt, a long stick was used, called an *oo*.

The cord and rope used on Niihau in early times were derived from many different plants. Ropes and nets were made of sennit, *puhala* roots, or pandanus, *makiukiu*, or Nihoa grass, *olona* and *malina*, or sisal. *Olona* was a trade item, but after sisal was introduced in the 1800s, the use of *olona* was discontinued. *Olona* was first soaked to decompose the pulp and then scraped with a shell. *Kaa* is the name for small, slender cord; *aho* is heavy cord.

Makau ✦ Fishhooks

An important tool developed by the people of old was the *makau*, or the fishhook, which was fashioned from bone, or *iwi*, wood, or *tumu*, and the most prized material, pearl, or *paua*, shell. The extensive travels and history of the ancient Polynesians can be studied through artifacts like the fishhook. According to Dr. Yosihiko Sinoto and Dr. Kenneth Emory in their book *Fish Hooks*, evidence has shown that certain types of fishhooks were discontinued before European contact.

The fishhooks of Niihau were often made of mother-of-pearl shells, which were rather uncommon in Hawaii. Between Kauai and Niihau is a reef ledge on which these special shells can be found. The Niihauans called the shell *paua*; it is approximately four inches in diameter. They used the shell for fishhooks and there are several good examples of Niihau shell fishhooks in private collections. When Dr. Sinoto examined one of these—

an intact mother-of-pearl fishhook found on one of the beaches on Niihau—he remarked that it appeared very unusual for Hawaii, resembling the fishhooks of Tahiti from the twelfth to eighteenth century. Mother-of-pearl fishhooks were scarce in the Hawaiian chain, he noted, except on Oahu and Kauai.

Na Mea Kaua ✦ Weapons & Self-Defense

Ancient weapons or *na mea kaua* were also important implements on Niihau. *Ihe* or highly-polished hardwood spears were fashioned by the men of Niihau from wood brought from Nihoa and Kauai. They also used the *loulu* palm for some battle spears. There was a spear called *alia*, but most were called the *ihe*. The types of spears were:

Ihe	spear, javelin
Ihe-laumeti	barbed spear
Ihe-o	sharp-pointed spear
Ihe-pahee	short spear
Ihe-pololu	long spear

The skill of spear throwing was called *kalii-oo-ihe*. Skill and courage were tested through spear throwing. Niihauans practiced mock attacks so they would be prepared when they went to war. The dagger or *pikoilua* was used in close combat. The dagger was about one foot in length and sharpened at one or both ends. Some had handles near the middle. Others had *olona* cord handles attached to the middle and wrapped around the wrist. Niihauans also had a spatula-like dagger of wood, the upper edge of which was completely surrounded by shark's teeth. This dagger also had a cord handle to secure it to the wrist. Sometimes handles were made from a dog's jawbone. This weapon was also used in the Hawaiian art of self-defense called *he lua*.

Almost all the men of Niihau in days of old were taught the Hawaiian art of self-defense. The people would attend schools for training. There the *kumu*, or teacher, would teach everything he knew, except for one particular hold, which was reserved for him—the *kumu lua*. It was not uncommon for a student to challenge the teacher, who indeed remained the teacher by reserving the one special hold! In 1834, there were two large schools. *Lua* experts were called *papakuialua*. *He lua* is no longer practiced on Niihau.

Panaiole was the ancient sport of shooting rats with the bow, or *kakakakikoo*, and arrow, or *panapua*. Although the warrior developed the skill of accuracy and concentration through the sport of *panaiole*, the bow and arrow were not used in warfare.

Waa ✦ Canoes

The canoes of old Niihau were about twenty-four feet in length. The bottom was formed of a single wood log, hollowed out to the thickness of 1 1/2 inches and shaped to a point at each end. The sides consisted of three boards, each about one inch thick. They were fitted and lashed to the bottom of the canoe. The canoes were narrow, and single canoes had outriggers called *ama*. The outriggers were shaped and fitted with the finest craftsmanship. Lashing together two canoes made a double canoe. Paddles were used, though some canoes had a light, triangular sail attached to a mast. This sail was usually made of woven *makaloa* mat. Ropes to lash boats and tackle for fishing were both made of *olona,* sennit, *makiukiu* and sisal, and were unusually strong and well-made. The Niihauans also had a special canoe of a single log polished to a sleek shine. Many of these were sixty feet long, 4 1/2 feet wide, and usually made of pine or redwood.

Due to winds and ocean currents, logs from the northwest coast of North America float to the shores of Niihau. Logs have been found in recent times since 1867, some of which have measured from four to six feet in diameter and sixty to eighty feet long. They arrive worn but well-preserved. It appears that the Douglas pine logs come from British Columbia, while the redwood logs come from California.

Na Mea Hana Lima ✦ Arts & Crafts

Niihauans remain methodical and particular in the arts and crafts. One of the unique crafts developed by the people of Niihau was the making of *ipu pawehe,* or decorated gourds, and the *umete pawehe,* or decorated food calabash. Since early times, these Niihau gourds and bowls have been treasured by visitors and islanders alike. Today, only a few remain intact in museums and private collections. They are no longer made.

The Niihauans call their design *pawehe,* regardless if the design is on a bowl, mat, gourd or as a body tattoo. The word *pawehe* pertains to anything with a decoration on it, and it is almost always a geometric design peculiar to Niihau. Ernest S. Dodge offers an account of the method of how the gourds were worked, told to him in 1940 by an old Niihau woman named Makahonuaumu. She said the gourds were stained while still green and the outer skin still quite soft. This skin was removed by scraping over the part that would carry the design. As the gourd dried, it changed color and hardened so that even a sharp object could not penetrate it. It is also said that sometimes before the gourd was picked off the vine, the design was etched into it. The Niihau gourds almost always have a light design on a dark background, though once in a while it is reversed. The gourds were grown on the southern side of the island near the shore.

Moena ✦ Makaloa Mats

The *moena pawehe* or decorated *makaloa* mats of Niihau were well-known in all Polynesia, although today the mats are no longer made. *Makaloa* mats are easily distinguishable from other mats because of their colorful geometric designs. The mats were of superior fineness and softness. Weaving was done exclusively by women. The art of weaving throughout the South Pacific reached its highest degree of skill on Niihau.

Niihau women used not only the *makaloa* for weaving but also *neki, loulu, hala* and *tohetohe*. Their mats were eagerly sought by visiting sailors and other islanders, and quite a trade was carried on. In 1861, the women were kept very busy weaving when a new fad hit Honolulu: *makaloa* hats. *Moena pawehe*, a reference to Niihau's mats, is a poetic expression often used about something of beauty or value.

Makaloa still grows at Lake Lalulu, Linakauhane, Kalanei and Papataale. The plant is a sedge that grows in brackish water. It is approximately one to six feet in height. Above the water line it is green in color while below the water line it is red to dark brown. There are three sheaths at the base of the true stem. These range in colors from light brown, red and purple to dark, brownish red. When these sheaths are removed, the true stem color ranges from white to a dark pink.

The preparation of the *makaloa* was done carefully since it is a delicate reed. The reeds were carefully dried, smoothed and put away until the weaver was ready to start her weaving. If the reeds were dried over a smouldering fire, it was called *olala*. If the mats were to be without a *pawehe* or design, it was called *pakea*. The weavers would go to the cave called Keanakoko to do most of their weaving. They put sand on the floor as a base and then covered the sand with coarse *lauhala* or pandanus mats. The work was very tedious, so tedious, in fact, that it took the weaver almost one year to complete a mat eighteen by eighteen feet. In the younger days of Alymer Robinson, the *makaloa* was carefully guarded and fenced to keep cattle from eating it. Alymer would have workers cut large *kiawe* branches to put over the growing reeds. This served both to keep the cattle from eating them and to provide a support for the *makaloa* during strong winds.

Tohetohe and *makaloa* often grow in the same pond and both are pollinated by wind. It was not unusual to see Niihau mats with red designs on one side, and red and green designs on the other. *Tohetohe* does not grow as tall as the *makaloa*, but it does have the red base. *Tohetohe* is a light green color. Another reed that grows in brackish ponds is *neki*. The *tohetohe* and *neki* were both used for mats.

As they were fragile, these mats were brought out only when special guests came. The mats were usually worked diagonally. A second design was formed on the surface by overlaying. Most of the designs were done in red, from the reed's sheath. Certain mats had unusual plaiting designs. This was also noted in Tahitian mats collected in Captain Cook's travels. Sometimes the plaiting changed at certain intervals to create other designs. The following are some poetic sayings about the *makaloa* mat.

O ko Kauwai moena kualana ua huilau ko laua me Niihau — "Kauai's famous mats are mixed up with Niihau's." Many Niihauans migrated to Kauai, taking with them their arts.

O ko Kauwai hoi, ua like no me ko Niihau — "Kauai is the same as Niihau."

A ahu ae i ka pawehe o Niihau ai la oe i ka manu o Kaula — "The mats of Niihau shall you wear and the birds of Kaula you will eat." Niihau alone is number one for the *alii*.

Moena e pahee ai koili — "The mat that glides on the skin." Softness.

There are some fine examples of the *makaloa* mats at the Bishop Museum in Honolulu and at Hulihee Palace in Kailua-Kona. A mat at the Bishop Museum was presented to the museum in 1923 by Princess Elisabeth Kalanianaole Woods. It measures nineteen by 26 1/4 feet. The edges are finished in an unusual double weft. The museum also has a mat that belonged to Bernice Pauahi Bishop. It is very fine with twenty-five wefts to the inch. This mat was worn by Kamehameha I as a cloak.

After the introduction by missionaries of quilting to Niihau, the women of the island turned their decorative talents to *kapa kuiki*, or Hawaiian quilting. Rather than using traditional *haole* or foreign designs, the Niihauans used designs from their own traditions. The Auckland Institute and Museum has the only known picture of an example of Niihau quilting. The design is unique to Niihau and not seen elsewhere in Hawaii.

Kii ✦ Petroglyphs

The unique designs used on Niihau quilts are also found in the many petroglyphs on the stone walls of Kaluamalu, Kaumuhonu Cave, Kii and elsewhere on limestone rocks.

According to the people of Niihau, petroglyphs were made by people from Tahiti. The old people say, "This is where all the people came from—from Tahiti—and they settled here on this island." In the old days, if you came from Niihau, you were called *kanaka Niihau*. If you came from Kauai or Maui, you were called *kanaka Kauai* or *kanaka Maui*. With the coming of the missionaries, it changed to *kanaka Hawaii*, all the peoples of the Hawaiian chain. Before this, Hawaii was not one. Each island stood alone!

Pupu ✦ Shells

Another one of the masterful crafts developed by the people of Niihau is the *lei pupu o Niihau*, the shell lei of Niihau. The island's most famous export item is now this exquisite Niihau shell lei. The *pupu o Niihau* is a dove-type shell only one-half inch in length. Turban and triton shells are also used in lei-making. The closest that most people can get to Niihau is to purchase and wear one of these rare beauties. It is the only shell lei in Hawaii that can be insured.

During the winter months, from December to May when the surf is high, these rare *pupu*, or shells, wash up on shore at several beach areas. They also wash onto other island shores in Hawaii, but not in such abundance as on Niihau. The only island where the shell is not found is on the island of Hawaii. When people notice the new crop of shells, it is not long before families are out on the beach, searching through the sand not only for the *momi*, but the true Niihau shell, the *kahelelani*. Shells are collected for months before the intricate lei-making begins.

The shells are sorted by size and shape, then graded. Only the best shells are used in the leis. Each shell is then given one or two holes (depending on the style of lei) by hand poking with a sharp instrument, usually a bicycle spoke. In the *pikake* style, there is a knot in the string between each shell. Some others are strung end to end, using from a single strand to five or more. This style is often called the *tutu lei*. The *kanelii* is the man's lei and is usually made of the larger shells. The *momi* and *laiki* shells are more abundant in winter, and the smaller *kahelelani* during May and June.

Some shells are cut at the tip and strung end to end, creating the multistrand sweetheart or *pololei* lei. These are usually exchanged at weddings. The *wili* lei, which is still being made, is very beautiful and extremely expensive because it is created using only the *kahelelani* shells. Another old style of lei is the *lei poepoe*. Other names include the *poleholeho* and *hale*. The *pikake* style of making a lei is a modern adaptation.

The names of the shells found on Niihau are:

white shell	*Momiokai*
yellow shell	*Lenalena*
spreckled shell	*Onikiniki*
rice shell	*Laiki*
blue shell	*Uliuli*
golden stripe	*Kahakaha*

The last two shells above are washed up on shore only two months in the year and are highly prized and valuable. The smaller shells are called *kahelelani* and are the true shells of Niihau. They come in a multitude of colors—the red and hot pink being the most prized. Other colors include dark brown and yellow, and the speckled pink, white, yellow, brown and red. Multicolored leis are called *kipona*. These are the most desired by the Niihauans and the most valuable. The multistrand *kahelelani* lei can range in price from a few hundred to several thousand dollars. Most of the homes on Niihau have large rice bags full of shells stored and waiting for grading, sorting and marketing. The money that comes from these tiny shells helps to supplement the islanders' meager salaries.

Leis were once made from *pukiawe* or black-eyed susan by the islanders. This smooth, slender vine grows well on Niihau and was used in making the *wili*-type leis. It is very beautiful in color—scarlet red with a black tip, with the more rare being solid black or white. It still grows there today, but the people have forsaken these seeds for the love of the *pupu o Niihau*.

Another beautiful shell found on Niihau, although not used in lei-making, is the land shell called *pupumoeone*. This land-snail shell is found only on Kauai and Niihau, in the large sand dunes far away from the ocean. The snail lives underground and its shell is particularly beautiful. It is a large, elongated shell, cream or brownish colored, and it is very distinct from land shells of other Hawaiian islands.

The shells of Niihau became world-known after "Song of the Islands" was composed by the Reverend Sam Kapu of Maui. Charles E. King's "Na Lei o Hawaii" made the shell the emblem of Niihau in May, 1923. The Hawaiian legislature, with the approval of Governor Wallace Rider Farrington, assigned flowers to each island as emblems; however, the *pupu o Niihau* became the emblem of Niihau.

Pupu o Niihau

Pupu o Niihau, auhea oe?	Where are you, oh shells of Niihau?
hoike a e oe a i kou nani.	Show your beauty.
He nani hiehie oi kelakela	A highly attractive beauty,
ka iini nui ia o kuu puuwai	A great desire in my heart.
Ho mai kou aloha a pili me au	Give of your love, let it embrace me
i koolua noho kahi mehameha.	Let us live together, alone.
I luna maua a o Haupu	We two upon Mount Haupu,
upu a e ke aloha nou, e ka ipo.	My love to you soars, oh sweetheart.
Haina ia mai ana ka puana	Let this story be told,
pupu o Niihau, auhea oe?	Where are you, oh shell of Niihau?

Reprinted by permission. Copyright Mileka Kanahele.

Na Mea Paani ✦ Sports

Historically, Niihauans had many games and sports: swimming, surfing, mock war games and sliding down the hill of Kawaihoa. They even had a game of marbles. Their marbles grew on shrubs—the seeds of the *kakalaioa* plant. The name of this plant means thorny, which it is. The shrub grows in rocky places on the lowlands. They called these marbles *kini kini*. Other sports included jumping rope, or *hake-okeo*, spear throwing, or *lono mataihe*, pole vaulting, or *ku pololu*, and an ancient gambling game, *pai*. Except for swimming, surfing and the children's game *kinikini*, these games and sports have not survived to modern times on Niihau.

Hoohelua or sliding was a sport enjoyed by all. The slides were located on the sides of Kawaihoa mountain. *Pili* and *malina* were used in place of a sled. Kaholuana is where the people went to participate in the sport of *hoohelua*. They would climb up the slopes of Kawaihoa, sit on the *pili* grass, raise their feet and slide down the mountain. Tutu Kaui mentioned that he had tried the slide at Kaholuana, and they now call this place Alawela. According to Kaui, he did not use *pili* grass, but used the leaves of the *malina* or sisal plant. He sat on the thickest part of the leaf, holding the points in his hands. It was a lot of fun, he said, but one must raise the legs up in the air while sliding down. Apparently there is a lot of sap in the leaf that makes it slide faster, but this sap also is irritating to the skin!

Hee Nalu ✦ Surfing

Surfing was also very popular among the people of old. Boards were about nine feet long and made of *wiliwili* or wood from the *ulu*. Sometimes they were stained black and rubbed down with coconut oil. There are several surfing areas on Niihau, beginning at Lana on the southwestern side and continuing north to Pakala. Several of these surfing areas, according to Tutu Kaui, have legends associated with them. For example, Lana was named after the legend of Lanaikahiki. Only those who lived there were experts. People from elsewhere did not know the peculiarities of the waves and ended up dashed against the rocks. There are large masses of submerged rocks, and there is no sand beach. When surfing a wave, one must know the precise moment to cut out or else risk being violently smashed upon the rocks.

The surfing place of Ohia is also treacherous. For some reason, the rider of the wave must cut out halfway to shore and then catch the wave behind in order to ride safely to shore. Unlike Lana, Ohia has a beach. The old people still say, "*Ohia nalu kaulana, pula maka a na kupuna*" — "Famous waves of Ohia that splashed in the eyes of our *kupuna*, our ancestors."

The offshore area called Kawahamana is located between Kaula rock and Lehua. There is a story about a surfer named Puuone whose boast was *"E keiki mai au no Kawahamana,"* or "I am the child (champion) of Kawahamana." It seems that his wife had left him for someone else. In his frustration, he went surfing. While he was surfing, the ocean suddenly became very rough; he had to paddle all around Niihau looking for a place to come ashore, aware that the people were watching him paddle about. He finally came to Kawahamana. The surfer was exhausted, but he wished to impress his wife so she would return to him. When he finally did catch a wave, he rode it all the way to shore, landing at Hapalua, which is close to Tahiu. He was cold and tired and when he reached the beach, his friends had a fire going to warm him. Because he was so brave, his wife returned to him. The following *mele* was composed about Puuone.

Puuone

A o oe ika lele pali *aohe e hoi ka wahine.*	If you lose a loved one and you jump over the cliff, your wife will not return.
A o oe ika hee nalu *aohe e hoi ka wahine* *make ka ili ike anu.*	If your wife leaves you and you surf to ease the frustrations, your wife will not return and you will die from the cold.
A o oe ika hula *hoi ka vahine ika poli o ke aloha.*	If you learn to dance the hula your wife will return to you.

In the surfing place known as Hualele, or "flying foam," there was a champion body surfer of this area named Laeanui. He was Tutu Kaui's grandfather. His boast was *"Keiki mai au, mai ka nalu o Hualele,"* or "I am the child, the champion, of the surf of Hualele." Other well-known surfing areas on Niihau are:

Kanaha Waho	Kalehua
Pueo Waho	Kawelo
Kamoilehua	Nanawaanu
Apu	Pakala
Lua	Kamoamoa
Kauhipahaku	

In the days of old, a contest of skill between the *alii*, or the royal persons, was held each October at the Kamoana surfing area. The celebration and surfing meet lasted for many weeks. There was a club formed that was called the Hui Nalu. The following song, *Ka Hui Nalu Mele*, was written for the surfing meet.

Ka Hui Nalu Mele
The Surf Club Song

He mele he inoa no ka hui nalu	A song, a name for the surfing meet,
haulani make kai o Kamoamoa.	and the restless seas of Kamoana.
Alawa ae oe ani kamakani	Softly blows the breeze as you glance,
moae kaulana no Kawaihoa.	the celebrated *moae* winds of Kawaihoa.
E aha ia ana kau aheahe	What, is this the time to be quiet?
me haaheo i kaili kai.	Cherish with pride the surface of the sea.
Aloha kahi nalu o Kamoamoa	Beloved is the wave of Kamoana,
ike ani peahi mehe ipo ala.	as it waves and beckons as if a loved one.
E kono mai ana la i kahi manao	It is inviting your desires to come
e pili meke kai hoeha ili.	and be with the sea that hurts your skin.
Ilihia i ka nani ke ike aku	Thrilled by the splendor that you see,
na pua hiehie a Kahelelani.	the regal children of Kahelelani.
Lia au i kala meka makemake	You have a yearning to be free,
kahi nalu hai mai o Kamoamoa.	but the waves of Kamoana will break you.
Hoohihi kamanao poina ole	Intertwined in my memory, I can't forget
ika papa hee nalu o ka muliwai.	the backwash that steals my surfboard.
Kohu kapa ahuula no Kamoamoa	Kamoana surf is likened to the red cloak,
hooheno ika ehu ehu o ke kai.	caressing power and the majesty of the sea.
Kai no paha oe ua i ke aku	The surf dances before you and you have
ia Lehua mokupuni ika ehu kai.	seen as the salt spray drifts upon Lehua.
He home noho ia na ke koolau	The home where the *koolau* wind resides,
poina ole ai kahi manao.	my longing for cannot be quenched.
Kohu lio kakela no Kamoana	Performing well on the horse of the ocean,
he pakika he pahee i ka ili kai.	gliding and sliding over the sea's surface.
Ua ana ia a ili wai like	You constantly struggle for breath,
na hana noeau a ka makua.	unlike the skillful deeds of our forefathers.
Oka milo hae no kau aloha	The furious curl is what is loved,
olali oke kai hanupanupa	gliding smoothly over the surface of the sea.
He manao no kou ae ike lihi	Desire compels me to surf the edge
ike kai popolo o ke ahiahi.	of the dark evening sea.
Akahi alana mai ka manao	I have this one floating thought,
e ike ika nalu ao Ohia.	to behold the waves of Ohia.
Alia hoi oe eka makemake	I have to wait, though I desire,
e ui lani nei paa ole iho.	it's beautiful but I can't catch it.
Ulu wehi wale ai o Kamoamoa.	Festively adorned is Kamoana,
i ka puni kauoha a na kupuna.	so deemed by the ancestors.
Nana i kono mai kahi manao	Kamoana has invited the idea
e ike ia kaleponi he aina hau.	of seeing California, land of ice.

Mea ole na ale o Kamoana *ka ilio hae o ka pakipika.*	The billows of the sea are insignificant, like the bark of a vicious dog of the Pacific.
Ke kiina iho ia ake akamai *a loaa mai au pahi koe pua.*	At the eyes' glance the expert knows, if you don't, the knife that scrapes will get you.
Nana inoi i nowelo aku *pau pono na ale o Kamoana.*	He has asked to search for wisdom, on all the waves of the sea.
Kilohi aku oe la oka nani *molina wai kula anapanapa.*	Gaze and behold the beauty of the gold glittering colored border.
Hea ia kou inoa o ka hui nalu *o ka hae Hawaii kou makia.*	Recited is your name, of the surfing club, the banner of Hawaii your purpose.
Haina kapuana ua lohe ia *kahi nalu hooheno o Kamoamoa.*	The song is ended, my story is told of the affection for the surf of Kamoana.

Hei ✦ String Figures

Another important amusement among the people of old was *hei*, or the art of manipulating string into figures. These figures always told a story and were usually accompanied by a chant as the craftsmen masterfully manipulated the string. Many of the chants and figures have been forgotten, but some remain known.

The most well-known string figure and chant from Niihau is of the water gourd of Kupoloula, chief of Niihau and the son of Kuhaimoana, whose ancestors were also Niihauans. Kupoloula drank of the sacred waters of Kupaoo. This *pohue*, or gourd, held the waters of life of the god Kane. It was hidden six month's journey toward the rising sun, in the hidden lands of Kane, more commonly known as Kanehunamotu. The *pohue* had been hidden in the bottom of a hole and the hole was guarded by Kanenaiau. The *pohue* was placed here by the brother of Pele, named Aukelenuiaiku. In order to bring life to his brothers, Kupoloula searched for and found the gourd. He broke the neck and cut up the *koko*, or netting, that held the *pohue*. The string figure is known as Hale o Kupoloula. Others know this figure as Huewai o Kupoloula. The word *pohue* is sometimes used for "water gourd" by Niihauans, though more commonly the word *huewai* is used. The chants that accompanied the act are included in *String Figures of Hawaii*, by Lyle A. Dickey. Niihau string figures include:

Nakuahele
Kuami
Waiu-o-ne (Breasts of Ne)
Tiputa ili o woka lale (The Noose of Walter Raleigh)
Toto o makalii (Small-Eyed Net)
Ka Naio (The Sandalwood Tree)
O Waiu o hinakeahi (Breasts of Hina)

Paliloa
Na waa Tiowea (Bird Canoe)
Pakii Lehua (Carved Lehua)
Pae Mahu (Hermorphodite)
Tuu tamahine (My Daughter)
Na Kanaka Alualu Kai (Men Who Chase the Sea)
Waa Lii Lii (Little Canoe)
Malo o Pua Ula (Red Fower Loin Cloth)
Upena (Fish Net)
Hale Paakai (House of Salt)
Hale o Taeo (Kaeo's House)
Uwala (Sweet Potato)
Weoweo
Holuana (Sledding)
Papio Makalii (Small-Eyed Papio Fish)
Huewai o Kaula (Water Gourd of Kaula)
Pali o Tee (Cliff of Kee)
Pakiki Lehua (Lehua is Tough)
Palai Huna Nui
Kauiti
Hale Loulu o Kane (Kane's Palm Leaf House)
Ka Ilio (The Dog)
Pai (a game)
Piko Ko Alii
Mooiti (Little Lizard)

The art of string figures is no longer practiced on Niihau. Like many other arts, crafts, skills and amusements, the life of the people of old was transformed by time, outside contact and neglect. These were but a few of the influences that followed the visit of Captain James Cook and the advent of the "historic" era.

CHAPTER IV

Niihau After Captain Cook

*Kaununui heiau kapu
noho ana ika poli o Kauwaha*

Kaununui possesses a sacred place Kauwaha,
which it cradles in its breast

Aerial of Kaumuhonu Bay. (*Photo: Bishop Museum*)

*K*APENA KUKE, as Captain James Cook was called by the people of Hawaii, first visited the island of Niihau in 1778 during his third voyage of exploration in the Pacific. His first impression of the Niihauans was that they spoke a very intelligible Tahitian language and that their physique and costume also resembled that of Tahiti. The native men, he wrote, were dressed in the *malo*, or loincloth, and the women wore Tahitian "pareu" or *pau*, a skirt.

As Cook stepped onto the beach, a chief of the island, Kaneoneo, began a ritual chant while the chief's attendants walked around the captain several times. Captain Cook noticed that the canoes were not of the large Tahitian type, nor were they carved as the ones from New Zealand, but they were nevertheless speedy and well-handled. It was also obvious that the natives practiced the art of *tautau*, or tattoo. The *alii*, the chiefs and royalty, looked splendid in their fine feather capes of red and yellow. On their heads were large feather helmets.

Cook's men noted at once the value of Niihau's fine *moena pawehe* mats. Recognizing that they could not be rivaled by those of other islands, several men took mats back to the ship. They particularly liked the designs of the mats. Cook noted that the people possessed small bits of *meti*, or iron, possibly from the sixteenth-century Spanish ships that previously visited Niihau or from wrecked vessels that may have floated to their shores.

Dr. William Ellis, assistant surgeon on Captain Cook's third expedition, would later draw some sketches of the grass houses he saw on Niihau. According to Peter Buck in *Arts and Crafts of Hawaii*, these drawings show gable roof lines without walls, resembling a tent's shape. Some homes had stone foundations. Cook stocked his ships, the *Resolution* and *Discovery*, with the *uhi*, or yam, *uwala*, or sweet potatoes, and the famous Niihau salt. In return, he left some gifts for the people: three goats, two pigs, pumpkins, onions and melon seeds. This was the **first** introduction of foreign plants and animals that would eventually alter the flora and fauna of Niihau.

There are stories on Niihau about visitors who had come to the islands long before Captain Cook's visit. These early visitors were called *Ehu* because of their red hair and fair skin. Legends suggest these foreigners settled in the Napali region of Kauai.

Although Kapena Kuke may not have been the first to visit Niihau, his contact with the people would lead to radical changes in the customs, manners and lifestyle of the Hawaiians over the next century. After Cook's voyage, Niihau became a destination for foreigners and merchants who would use the island for obtaining fresh provisions.

Emigrations

The most tragic consequence of this new foreign contact on Niihau was the increasing decline of the native population. At the time of Cook's visit, the number of Hawaiians on the island was estimated to be a sizable 10,000. Because of drought or other reasons, there were many migrations of people from Niihau to Kauai in the 1700s. Around 1800, there was another mass migration from Niihau to the island of Kauai, mainly to the Kalalau and Nuololo (Nualolo) Valleys, and to the Haena, Hanalei, Waimea and Kekaha areas. Only 4,000 natives were estimated to be left on the island.

Later, the population was further decreased due to the introduction of foreign diseases and the policy changes of the Sinclairs, new owners who purchased Niihau in 1864. Before the purchase, Niihauans largely raised dogs for food. But since the Sinclairs intended to use the island for cattle and sheep ranching, they ordered that all the dogs be killed to protect the new livestock. Many islanders refused to kill their animals and so they migrated to Lehua and Kauai. The dwindling size of the native population of Niihau is sadly reflected in the following census figures:

1778:	10,000 *kanaka*		1841:	1,000 *kanaka*
1800:	4,000 *kanaka*		1864:	1,008 *kanaka*
1833:	1,079 *kanaka*		1868:	300 *kanaka*

The decline of the Hawaiian population was compounded by fundamental changes in land tenure. Niihau was originally monarchy land except for some small parcels. Following the Great Mahele of 1848, when the lands of the Hawaiian Kingdom were divided into royal, government and common lands, the Niihauans tried to purchase or lease their property. Two natives received lands in the Great Mahele while many others negotiated leases with the Hawaiian government. However, in 1858 a new government agent raised the leases to unheard-of prices, making it necessary for natives to move to Kauai.

Friends on Kauai tried to help these dispossessed Niihauans by sending letters of protest to the Minister of Interior. Numerous letters from Niihauans Puko, Kauukualii and Wahineaea that requested leasing rights or purchase for Niihauans are preserved in the Hawaii State Archives. An 1855 letter from King Kamehameha IV indicates that he agreed to sell the land to the people, but he later died and it was sold it to the Sinclairs.

Sale of Niihau

The major transfer of Niihau's land ownership came in 1864 when the Sinclair family purchased the island. The prime force behind the purchase was Eliza McHutchenson Sinclair, a pioneering woman who seemed to yearn for a home away from civilization where she could live with her family in the old matriarchal style. She was the wife of Captain Francis Sinclair, who in 1840 moved his family from Craigforth, Scotland, to New Zealand, where their first home was at Pelone Beach. The land Captain Sinclair purchased at Wanganui had to be abandoned because of trouble with the Maoris. Pigeon Bay was their next New Zealand home, far away from other white people.

After the death of Captain Sinclair, the iron-willed Mrs. Sinclair took her family on to Tahiti, Honolulu and British Columbia, and then California. While voyaging to California, their ship was blown off course and in 1863 they landed for a second time in Honolulu. Deciding to settle in the islands, she purchased a home on the plains now known as Makiki, on Oahu, and her sons began negotiations for the purchase of Niihau.

These negotiations were initiated in September, 1863, when sons James McHutchenson Sinclair and Francis Sinclair offered the government $6,000 for the island. The Hawaiian Minister of the Interior, G.H. Robertson, responded that the the island could be leased or purchased for $10,000. Appraisals of Niihau were conducted by four individuals: Valdemar Knudsen, who placed the value at $6,000, Dr. Smith ($7,500), George Rowell ($7,500) and G. H. Weideman, who priced the island the highest at $10,000. On January 20, 1864, the government sold the island of Niihau for $10,000 to the Sinclairs, with the exception of the two *ahupuaa* of Halawela and Kahuku, sold to Iosia Koakanu, and fifty acres that had already been sold by the government to an individual named Papapa. (See Royal Grant in Appendix.) Kamehameha V issued the following statement when Niihau was deeded to the new "*haole* kings":

> The natives are yours and you are the new chief, and they will work and serve you according to the laws and customs of the King of Hawaii. They are subject to this rule only—if it does not interfere with the people's rights of a grant of a little land to plant food, a place for a home, firewood and the right to fish their waters.

When the people of Niihau heard that the island was being negotiated for sale to *haole malihini*, or foreign newcomers, they again urged the government to sell the land to them as promised by King Kamehameha IV. (See Appendix for their letters.) After the Sinclairs were deeded the land, many disappointed islanders migrated to Oahu, Maui and Kauai.

Koakanu

The native family that retained control of a large portion of Niihau were the Koakanus, who had applied for a royal grant during the Great Mahele in 1848. Koakanu's *ahupuaa* of well over 2,000 acres ran across the best tracts of the island at two different places. One parcel of Koakanu's land, Halawela, lay across the heel part of the island (Niihau is shaped like a foot); the other parcel, Kahuku, was in the mountains. Papapa's fifty acres (patent issued 1855), were at Kamalino and Omaumalua.

Since the new owners had acknowledged the royal grant of Koakanu, they did the best they could to work around the Koakanu property. However, since the Koakanu couple was not employed by the Sinclairs, they made life a little difficult for the Sinclairs. Every fence or road that the Sinclairs wished to build crossed Koakanu's land and Koakanu would not permit access. If the Sinclairs wanted to cross Koakanu's lands to fish, they had to go inland to avoid Koakanu's land, since the water in the ocean also belonged to the *ahupuaa*. The Sinclairs offered to purchase all of Koakanu's land holdings. Koakanu emphatically said no. Finally, the eldest son, James Sinclair, figured a way to resolve the problem. He sent for a man that was loved by the Niihauans, Valdemar Knudsen, or "Kanuka." He told Valdemar to offer $1,000 in shiny new trade dollars for Koakanu's land.

Valdemar made the trip to the home of the Koakanus. He talked for many hours before he mentioned the offer from the Sinclairs. Again and again, Koakanu said no, he didn't want to sell. Knudsen took out the bag of dollars and placed it on the table. Koakanu again said no. Finally, Knudsen emptied the bag of bright trade dollars on the table. Koakanu's wife was fascinated by seeing so much money and begged her husband to reconsider. He again said no. After many hours, Valdemar was about to give up. He started to put the dollars back into the bag when the wife again urged her husband to sell. His resistance weakened and he agreed. Valdemar returned to the Sinclairs with good news.

Three months after their initial purchase, the family now owned the two *ahupuaa* of Koakanu. The entire island cost them $11,000. It is not known what Koakanu did with the trade dollars, but it is believed that he moved to Koloa, Kauai. However, it is interesting to note that when Koakanu's deed was recorded on March 7, 1864, Koakanu received only $800 from James and Francis Sinclair. Valdemar Knudsen acted as the notary public on the recording of the deed from the Koakanu to the Sinclairs. The new owners immediately completed occupancy of Niihau, living first at Kaununui and then building a permanent house on a plateau at Kiekie. This second house had a magnificent view and was called Hale Kawaihoa because it faced Kawaihoa. The ridge that the house sits upon has an unusual air current that brings more gentle trade winds and showers to this area than anywhere else on the island.

"Mama Luahine," as Mrs. Sinclair was called, quickly found Niihau too isolated, so she made another land purchase on Kauai. By 1868 or 1869, she had completed negotiations to obtain Makaweli on Kauai. This is where she spent the last years of her life living in a matriarchal fashion surrounded by her family. To her very last days, she retained her independence and strength. She remained sharp-minded and never relinquished control of family matters. She also rode her horse almost to the end. Mrs. Sinclair died at the age of 92.

Mrs. Sinclair's sole heir became her grandson, Aubry Robinson, or as he was called by the Niihauans, "Opale Lopikana." Aubry was born in New Zealand on October 17, 1853. He attended Boston University Law School and was admitted to practice in 1875. He traveled for seven years before he came back to Kauai to attend to the business.

Like all generations of Sinclairs and Robinsons, Aubry took an active interest in the church and missionary work. He was a generous contributor to the church and was known to take roll call on Sundays! The attitude of the Sinclairs toward the natives was highly patriarchal—they treated Hawaiians as children, not *kauwa* or slaves. Aubry Robinson would, however, eventually demand feudal service from the natives, and at his beckoning, all the available native population came forth. Whenever the *kanaka* heard that Robinson was coming to visit, as a show of respect they would put on the finest clothes they owned. The women came in colorful *muumuu* and the men wore white shirts.

Some outsiders visited privately-owned Niihau by invitation in the nineteenth century. One such visitor wrote that in 1867 he visited the Pahau *heiau* at Kawaihoa, and at Nonopapa he noticed a wall of shingle built as though it were a sea wall to protect the island from *Kona* winds. This wall ran out to a point northeast of the Nonopapa landing. Nonopapa was the main trade depot, with four *halepili*, or thatched buildings, and one *halepili* warehouse, none of which still stand. Queen Liliuokalani also visited Niihau in 1891 aboard the ship *James McKee*. It is reported that the islanders gave her an appropriately royal welcome.

In spite of these few visits, after the Robinsons took ownership, the island of Niihau gradually slipped into a self-imposed isolation. Contact with the outside world dwindled while ranch life and the church reshaped island lifestyles. Indeed, one of the most important forces to influence islanders in the 1800s was Christianity. After the 1820s, through the efforts of *haole* Protestant missionaries, Niihauans were converted to Christianity. Between 1823 and 1824, it was proclaimed by Kalanimoku and Kaahumanu that Niihau and all the other islands would observe the Sabbath and keep it holy. All unnecessary work was forbidden, as well as murders, thefts and fighting. The chief of Niihau carried this a bit further and prohibited drunkenness.

Hale Pule ✦ Church & Religion

The Church of Niihau was associated with the O Waimea Hawaiian Church on Kauai. Although the Waimea Church is still considered the mother church, on July 15, 1866, the church on Niihau separated itself from the Kauai congregation. The deacon at that time was M. Kauohai, and the church was named the Church of Niihau. On Sundays, services were held at the Government School House in Puuwai, and on weekday evenings, services were conducted at the home of John Kapahee, who lived in Nonopapa, where a majority of the members lived. A Wednesday night meeting was for women only; evening meetings on Thursday were for everyone. The meetings consisted of readings from Biblical passages, followed by discussions of their meanings. Committing the verses to memory was a favored activity. In 1868, D. S. Kupahu became deacon of the Church of Niihau; in 1870, A. Kaukau became deacon.

At the time of the founding of the Church of Niihau, there were two other denominations on the island—a sect following the Reverend Rowell of Waimea, Kauai, and the Roman Catholic Church. By 1868, there were five different denominations on Niihau: Mormons, Roman Catholic, Kanepalaka religion, Reverend Rowell followers and the Church of Niihau. By 1890, however, the Church of Niihau began gathering most of the population as members.

Hosana

1 Ua mau mai e ka pono
mai kamakua lani mai
ke hui nei kakou
I kona lokomaikai.

hui Hosana ia ke akua
mana lani kiekie
kawa iho ana mai
I ko kakou ola.

2 E hui mai kakou
makua me keiki
lokahi pu kamano
I hookahi puuwai.

3 E ia no makou
ke mele oli aku nei
maka ino oka Haku
Iehowa Sapaota.

4 E ala like nahoa
e palio no ka pono
e mau eke kupaa
ma ka pono oka uhane.

5 Kaulana keia hui
mana hana oka pono
oka hui Kula Sapati
o Kalawelonaakala.

6 E ia kakou apau
ia koakoa mai nei
e ike ina hana
kaulana o Iubile.

7 Ena hoa luhi nei
e hoola na kamano
maka pono o kauhane
e ola ai kakou.

8 Hookahi no makia
nana i kuhikuhi mai
na hana e ulu ai
kapono no kakaou.

9 Nana i alakai ae
Ia kakou apau
meke ao malamalama
oka Lanikila mau.

10 Hauoli pu kakaou
I keia la maikai
hoi Kulasapati
o Kawelonaakala.

Written by M.W. Kaaneikawahale Keale.
Recorded under the name **Ua Mau** by Moe Keale. Translation unavailable.

Keale

In 1912, Moses W. Kaaneikawahaale Keale, or Keale Ta Kaula (Keale the Prophet), opened the doors of his new church Iubile, the one and only church structure on Niihau. The religion of the church was Hoomana Ia Iesu, derived from *Kalawina,* or Calvinism. The large, one-room church still exists on the foundation of an older church and is situated majestically in a large yard. Surrounding the church are twenty-five stone plaques, each naming the head of a family on Niihau at the time the church was completed in 1912. Twelve stone plaques are on one side of the church, thirteen on the other. The thirteenth plaque commemorates Keale Ta Kaula and is inscribed "Luna Ona Ohana Pau Loa." The cornerstone faces the east and it has the insignias of Keale's religion carved upon it.

Keale is considered by Niihauans to have been a powerful Christian *kahuna,* a prophet and a miracle-worker with divine gifts. He was descended from a remarkable genealogy: the Keales were large (over six feet tall), strong and very bright. Many tales are told of adventures requiring their strength, skill and fearless bravery. In the 1700s, some of the family moved with many others from Niihau to Kauai in a mass migration. Their home became Kalalau, where they had large land holdings. They later returned to Niihau.

Keale was born at Kalalau, on Kauai, about 1828 and grew up to become a very good hunter, climbing the cliffs in the valley in pursuit of game. It is said he was as sure-footed as a goat and that anywhere the goats could go, he would follow. As a young man, Keale was not one who believed in the new Christian religion. One day while he was hunting goats, chasing them all over the cliffs, he noticed one particularly beautiful white goat and set off to capture him. As he climbed a cliff trying to catch the goat, it disappeared! In his quest for the game, he hadn't noticed that he had wandered onto a ledge that had no way up or down. There are two different versions of what happened at this point. The first is that a rock dropped from above and hit him. As he fell, he cried out, "God save me!" He landed in the river below and his dog pulled him out to the riverbank, where he revived. When he awoke, he stood up and gave thanks to God for saving his life. The second version is that when he fell or jumped, and not being a religious man, he called, "If there *really* is a God, he will save me and I shall spend the rest of my life serving him." Keale's fall was broken as he fell into a *puhala,* or pandanus, and then into a section of the Kalalau river called Makani Kahao. It is said that there was no breath in him when his dog pulled him from the river. The dog licked his face until he started to breathe again. After he was revived, Keale picked up a rock and set it upon a large boulder as a monument, naming it *Ke Ola Ke Akua* (The Life of God). Tutu Kaui worked in Kalalau Valley as a cowboy when he was a young man with Kauhi Hookano, foreman of Makaweli Ranch, and Shima Kapahu, a cowboy, who first showed him the monument.

After Keale was saved, he left Kalalau and moved to Waimea, Kauai, where he started his first church. He called this church Lanakila. Then God led Keale to Niihau. He moved to an area called Kamalino where he built another church and again named it Lanakila. He built his home nearby at Paweo and, as he finished, he called all the people to come and live in the area. He said, *"Pii katai mao maa nei a puni o Niihau, aole pii ia keia kahua hale, e ke kai"* — "The seas will touch everywhere on this island on Niihau, but will never come up here to my house." This prophecy has remained true until today. Not one drop of water touched Paweo during Hurricane Iwa in 1982.

Keale was worshipped like a god by the people. They came to him for all answers. He was indeed a prophet and *kahu*, or minister, and he was so loved and respected by the people that they wrote many songs in his honor. He in turn wrote hymns and prayers for his church, which are used today.

At instructions from God, Keale moved his church to an area known as Kauanaulu. He then changed the name of the town to Puuwaialohaokaohana, now shortened to Puuwai. His church, established in 1896 at Puuwai and called Lanakila, was a tent and Kaomea was the first *kahu*. A new church was built on that site and also called Lanakila. Keale's fourth and final church on Niihau—Iubile—was completed in January, 1912, and remains the only church on the island today.

Edward Manase Kahale was Keale's best friend, and he built the limestone cornerstone for Iubile. Kahale had wanted to leave Niihau, but Keale did not want him to go, so he put him to work carving the cornerstone to Keale's design. When Kahale finished his task, Keale informed him that Kahale would never leave Niihau, as the new church would hold him there. Kahale died in 1939, never having left Niihau.

Though Keale lived in Paweo, he knew just who did and who did not attend church in Puuwai. He continued to instruct the *kahu* on the procedures to be followed. Keale would be at home in Paweo when all of a sudden he would tell his wife to cook food, as someone was going to come. Sure enough, two hours later, someone came to seek help from him. He was considered a *kahuna makaula*, or prophet. Keale was so powerful that when he found out some people were still worshipping in the ancient way and praying to idols, he immediately went to Keanahaki Cave and prayed. It is said the cave cracked and split in half, closing off that entire section of the ancient religious temple. Because of this event, the cave to this day is called Keanahaki, or The Split Cave. This was the largest cave on Niihau.

Other legends are still told of Keale's spiritual powers. Kaluaakona was the home site of a *kupua* or demigod who lived during the time of Keale. The man's name was Kaimi and he was a sorcerer. On this spot, Kaimi told the people of Niihau, "When I die you *must* bring my body back to this place." But Keale had the ability to see into the future and he did not like what he saw. He called the people of Niihau together and told them, "No, do not bring this man back to this spot, because if he was to return, he would live again. Wherever he dies, bury him there." On another occasion, Keale's foresight warned him that the most powerful *kahuna anaana*, or sorcerer, of Molokai was coming to Niihau to challenge him. Keale planned to meet him on the beach when his canoe landed. As the two met, the *kahuna* from Molokai offered Keale a smoke on his pipe ("If he lit his pipe and offered it to you and you smoked it, you would die"). Keale stared intently at this *kahuna*, took the pipe and smoked it. He did not die. After smoking the pipe, he offered it to the *kahuna* and said, "Now you smoke, and after you smoke you had better leave my island or you will die." The *kahuna* smoked his own pipe, set sail in his canoe and died on his trip home.

> *E hiki mai ana ka la* The day will come
> *E huli ana ke alo o Niihau ilalo* when the face of Niihau will be
> *A o kekua iluna.* turned down and its back up.

(*The kaona* or hidden meaning: One day the people will turn from the teachings of their *kupuna*, their ancestors. That day will be the Niihauans fall in disfavor. Predicted by the religious leader Keale in 1917.)

School

Keale established a strong tradition of *pule* or prayer on Niihau, and the church also played a major role in public education. The island's first public school was built in 1900; the first schoolmaster was Edward M. Kahale, deacon of the church.

When Kumu Kula Edward Manase Kahale unexpectedly died in 1939, the community was suddenly left without a teacher. While few of the people had the education required to teach, Mrs. Miriam Keale Hanaiki Niheu, educated at Iolani Girls School in Honolulu, and Mrs. Hannah K. Niau, educated at the public school in Kekaha, Kauai, were available. Both spoke beautiful English. Mrs. Hanaiki Niheu taught grades 1 through 3 and Mrs. Niau taught grades 4 through 6.

Entering the Twentieth Century

As Niihau slowly entered the twentieth century, the size of the tiny Hawaiian community remained small. Although the following figures do not include Niihauans living and working off the island, the population has consistently stayed below three hundred:

1900:   172 *kanaka*   1960:   254 *kanaka*
1920:   191 *kanaka*   1980:   226 *kanaka*
1940:   182 *kanaka*

As small and remote as Niihau is, the island has not been able to totally ignore events and developments elsewhere. In 1919, four Niihau men joined the military to serve their country in the First World War: Keala Hunamana, Kaahakila Kalimahuluhulu, Liwai Peleiholani and Salowana Robinson. The *ohana* of Niihau gathered at the church to pray for their safe return from the war. Among those who went to pray were Malaki Kanahele, Akaneki Pomaikai, Kaua Keamoai, Piilani Nohokula, Ema Kaahakila, Laisa Mikiki and Alika Robinson.

During the 1920s and 1930s, economic difficulties on Niihau forced some islanders to leave. Although the famous Niihau *pawehe* mats were still being made in 1922, they didn't provide a significant economic income to the weavers. In 1924, many of the Niihau males left, lured away by the higher wages earned as stevedores on steamers.

When a severe drought hit the island in 1930, the community suffered harsh conditions. The drought not only dried up the reservoir, but it took a heavy toll on the cattle, horses and sheep and weakened the surviving livestock. The drought finally ended on August 3, 1931, when a five-inch rainfall filled all the lakes and reservoirs.

December 7, 1941

After December 7, 1941, Niihau was pulled dramatically into the Second World War. Niihauan Howard Hawila Kaleohano (formerly of Kona, Hawaii) was in an outhouse when a Japanese pilot nearly crash-landed his plane on top of the outhouse. Maintaining his presence of mind, he captured the pilot and confiscated his papers, which would eventually help to break the Japanese communications code. However, after losing his papers, the pilot escaped and then made continued attempts to retrieve his documents from Hawila. For a week, the Niihauans signaled to Kauai for help and received no answer, unaware that Kauai was under a blackout.

Hawila decided to take the boat *Minehaha* and cross the choppy channel to Kauai. Five men accompanied Hawila on the trip: Kekuhina Kaohelaulii, Akana Kaohelaulii, Willie Kaohelaulii, Kahokuloa Kanahele and Enoka Kaohelaulii. The men left Niihau at 1:30 a.m. and reached Waimea at 3:20 p.m. on December 13, 1941. While Hawila was thus engaged, Benjamin Kanahele managed to kill the Japanese pilot after being shot himself by the pilot several times. Major General George F. Moore, Commanding General of the Middle Pacific, pinned the Medal of Merit and the highest military award given a civilian—the Medal of Freedom—on

Hawila. Benjamin Kanahele received the Medal of Merit and the Purple Heart from Lieutenant General Richardson for courageously killing the pilot, even though Kanahele was unarmed and had been shot three times.

Thus ended the famous "Battle of Niihau."

The arrival of American troops on Niihau in 1943 further transformed the once-isolated island. There were no modern amenities on Niihau before the troops landed. For the first time the people experienced jeeps, radios, beer and electricity. The troops were mostly from Kauai, an island unit of infantry. They brought with them four jeeps, a motor car and cases of beer.

For nearly thirty years after World War II, the Hawaii territorial and state governments made several attempts to purchase Niihau outright, arguing that the island was in danger of becoming "tourist owned." Investigations were conducted by the government that claimed the people were "unhealthy and uneducated." Finally, in 1970, Governor William Quinn asked for immediate state action in the purchase. At this point, the Niihau people responded by pleading, "Please, no change. Leave us alone." Senate committees, concerned about the health of the people, were told by Niihauans, "Clean up Honolulu before trying to change us." In 1980, several more attempts were made to purchase Niihau. The people's wishes prevailed: "We prefer our present mode of life. Please leave us alone." They didn't want their way of life altered.

Today, there is one public school on Niihau for grades 1 through 8. The 1980 census shows there were forty-six pupils at the school on Niihau, with three teachers who are natives of Niihau: Jean Kuuleialoha Kelly Keale, Blossom Kanahele and Abigail Kaohelaulii Shintani. The teachers are employed by the Department of Education. The children usually go on to high school on Kauai at Waimea High School, or on Oahu at the Kamehameha School. Students who continue their education off the island generally prefer to return to Niihau to live, even after their exposure to a more modern life style. Although the men are employed by the Robinson family in their business operations, some families are supported by social welfare in time of crisis or financial need. In October, 1986, 176 island residents were subsidized by public funds or received some sort of government aid such as welfare. Overall, their health is excellent. When a medical emergency arises, the person is sent to Kauai for treatment at the Robinsons' expense.

The love that the people of Niihau have for their community and way of life is perhaps difficult for outsiders to understand. They have learned to put their neighbors, family and friends before themselves. When Hurricane Iwa totally destroyed the main school house and church on Niihau in 1982, the community bonded together to act. First they repaired their church, then they rebuilt the school. Only after the places for worship and learning were repaired did they restore their own homes. Such is life on Niihau.

Iubile Church after repairs to damage from 1982 hurricane. (*Photo: Reri Tava*)

CHAPTER V

The Way of Life on Niihau

*Na keiki lawaia o ka aina
ahe kama eu no na kiu eiwa*

The fisherman of the land,
the child of the nine *kiu* winds

Niihau residents outside their homes, 1890. (*Photo: Bishop Museum*)

THE PEOPLE OF NIIHAU are still close to the land, ocean and sky. Their simple lifestyles do not heavily rely on technology and consumerism. The food on their table is not completely supplied by the supermarket. Nature is not discovered by mowing the lawn, putting a plant in the window or taking a weekend outing. Entertainment is not wholly dependent on electronic media or fancy gadgets.

Instead, the Niihauan looks to the plants and animals of the earth, the fish and seaweed of the sea and the religious spirit of their music and art to sustain and uplift their uncomplicated lives. The plants and agricultural produce of Niihau are used for many purposes, including sale, personal food and *laau*, or medicine.

Ko ✦ Sugar Cane

Niihau once produced a large quantity of sugar cane, pineapple and bee honey. The place where sugar cane was first grown is between Waihonu and the pine groves in Halalii. This area also provided a good, sweet water suitable for drinking. There once was a house in this area that was owned by Aubry Robinson and used for fishing purposes. When he began staying there on fishing trips, the first sugar cane crops were being cultivated. He therefore placed a *kapu* on the plant so that it would multiply.

The sugar cane at Halalii grew near a great number of sand dunes, which the winds frequently shifted from place to place. As the sugar cane would grow, the constant winds caused it to lay down. As the winds continued to blow the sand, it covered the cane stalks, leaving only the leaves exposed above the sand, while the cane itself continued to grow beneath the sand to almost twelve feet long. If one did not know that the cane was growing underground, one might pull only the front end off and cut off a short piece of cane.

The people of Niihau, knowing that the cane was growing under the sand, would get down and dig with their hands, following the cane to the end of the stalk to get the whole cane. Thus, the name for the cane, *Ko eli lima o halalii*, or sugar cane dug by hand. The cane is no longer growing at Halalii.

Halakahiki ✦ Pineapple

Although it no longer grows on Niihau, the *halakahiki*, or pineapple, grew better on Niihau than on other islands. They were much smaller than the present species and the inside was orange-colored. The taste of the Niihau pineapple was very sweet and juicy. These pineapples were of the Tahitian variety, brought to Niihau from the Marquesas Islands in the early 1800s. Behind Kiekie on the plain toward the mountain range were many natural pineapple fields. Pineapple grew all over the island spontaneously, cultivated only by nature. The largest natural plantation was on the northeast side near Kii. If Niihau had a more favorable altitude, *halakahiki* might have become the island's most important commercial crop.

Hone ✦ Honey

The bee culture and honey products of Niihau are a successful agricultural export. When bee culture was first introduced on Niihau, a Japanese man named Ishimatsu Shintani was head beekeeper. Shintani was born in Japan and immigrated to Kauai as a sugar plantation laborer. Shintani later married a Niihau woman who persuaded him to return with her to Niihau. Under Shintani's supervision, honey production became a significant source of income to Niihau. The honey is placed in 55-gallon drums and exported around the world. Approximately 1,200 cases (eighty tons) are shipped annually along with several tons of wax.

Laau ✦ Medicine

The use of plants for *laau*, or medicine, has an ancient heritage on Niihau and continues to help supplement western medical care. The following folk remedies are still in use on Niihau:

Pilo, or Hawaiian Spider Lily. The root is pounded, mixed with salt, then applied to the affected area. It is never placed on an open wound.

Hialoa. Young plants are uprooted and the *lepo* is removed. The bark of the root is then removed. They are cut into sections and chewed. Used for sores in the throat. Bitter tasting.

Banana blossom. The flower end of the banana stock is cut off and the sap that gathers from the cut is used for sores in the mouth. Very bitter.

Koali. The roots are pounded into a poultice and applied to broken bones.

Ka liko. Made into a tea which acts as an enema.

Hone, or honey. Used as a covering for burns.

Kai, sea water. Used as a cathartic. For sore throats and as a cure-all.

Paua, a bi-valve shell. Juice from the inside of the shell is used for baby's thrush throat.

Laau Kahea. Prayer form of medicine. These medicines are given along with prayers of forgiveness, or *pule kala*.

Onikiniki, or crab. The eyes of this crab are pounded and used as a cure for sore throat.

Kupala (*uhi*). Acts like epsom salts, a cathartic, on the bowels. For constipation and dysentery. Young leaf buds are fed to pregnant women at birth to hasten delivery of the child.

Pia. Mixed with salt and *alaea*. A treatment for dysentery.

Ilima. The juice from freshly-squeezed *ilima* blossoms is given to pregnant mothers at birth. The juice acts as a cathartic and helps make delivery easier.

Makaloa. Used as the strainer for medicines. The reed is crushed first.

Hinahina. Tea is made out of the dried *hinahina* and used in the treatment of diabetes.

Uwala. Certain types are used. For sore throats, squeeze the juice from a raw potato and gargle.

Laau mimi paa. For inability to urinate, take a handful of *makaloa*, gather eight young shoots of ti, and one small piece of *alaea* clay. Pound these together well and strain the juice. Take two times a day, morning and night. You must take this medicine for several days. Drink a lot of water to flush out the body. Do not digest any saltwater or salty foods.

To, or sugar cane. For tiredness. Take the sugar cane stalks. Pound them, strain the juice and drink.

Halakahiti, or pineapple. Used for many diseases.

Laau no ka apu noni. For one dosage: four ripe *noni*, two white sugar cane sections, one-half coconut (soft meat), one sweet potato. Pound all of these together, then strain. Add a pinch of salt, place in a pot and bring to a boil. Let cool, then drink the juice. Don't forget to say a prayer before you drink this. If there are two persons needing medicine, double the dosage.

Laau hoomaemae koko. For blood cleansing. Take a handful of *kaunaoa* and boil in sweet water. Strain and store in container. When you are thirsty, drink this instead of water. Take this potion for three days and rest. After three days, you may drink fresh water. Be sure to keep *kaunaoa* in a damp bag so it remains cool and will not dry up.

Laau ono ana mai like ole. For hemorrhage, high blood pressure. *Alaea* clay or stone is this medicine. There are two types of *alaea: eleele*, black and hard; *ula ula,* red and soft. Scrape the two into a powder until you have about one teaspoon. Mix with a glass of water and drink. These are the different diseases for which you can use this: *heekoko,* or hemorrhage, *koko pii,* or high blood pressure, *no ka nae nae,* or asthma, and *luae koko,* or vomiting blood.

Laau he apu. For rest, mental relaxation. Take three sections white sugar cane, one piece of soft coconut meat, one spoonful *alaea* powder, one sweet potato. Pound these together, mixing well. Put mixture in a pot and bring to a boil. Strain and let cool, add a pinch of salt, then drink the juice. When taking this medicine, do not drink water for one hour. Also, don't forget to *pule,* or pray, before taking this medicine.

Hi hoonau. For diarrhea. The flowers of the *hialoa* plant are the medicine. Find a patch of *hialoa* and pick a handful of blossoms. Chew the blossoms and swallow. They will dry up when swallowed, feeling like sandpaper as they go down the throat. There are no restrictions on food or water.

Hua & Laau ✦ Vegetables & Plants

The *hua,* fruits and vegetables, that might be found today on Niihau include both plants brought by ancient Hawaiians and those introduced by foreigners in the last two hundred years. These *hua* include:

uwala	sweet potato	*manako*	mango
to	sugar cane	*ohialoke*	rose apple
maia	banana	*palama waiu*	plum
niu	coconut	*ipu*	melon
niu kahiki	dates	*pu*	pumpkin
ulu	breadfruit	*akakai*	onion
taro	kalo	*lemiliilii*	calamondin
tuawa	guava	*halakahiki*	Tahitian pineapple
alani	orange	*hei*	papaya
uhi	yam		

The *tumu* and *laau,* trees and plants, of Niihau are also varied:

kiawe	mesquite	*manienie*	Bermuda grass
hala	pandanus	*koali*	morning glory
paina	ironwood	*kakalaioa*	gray nickers
niu	coconut	*malina*	sisal
wiliwili	native tree	*pili*	grass
ulu	breadfruit	*ti*	shrubby plant
naio	sandalwood	*loulu*	palm
papipi	cactus	*popolo*	parasitic vine
lauae	fern	*pikake*	jasmine flower

pukanawila	bougainvillea	*tiare*	Tahitian gardenia
pulupulu	cotton	*noni*	mulberry
melia	plumeria	*kuikui*	candlenut tree
aloalo	hibiscus		

Snacks

The Niihauians enjoy several snacks that are found among the vegetation of their island. The *papipi* or cactus fruit is eaten when ripe. It is peeled and eaten right off the cactus. This cactus is known elsewhere as *panini*. The cacti have sliver-like spurs that become embedded deep into the skin when touched. Children are taught to brush the fruit off with a branch before picking it. Another snack is provided by the *havana*, which are the *loulu* palm seeds. The seeds from this palm taste like coconut and are eaten raw. Children on Niihau also enjoy chewing the mature *kiawe* beans. When they are boiled in water, the beans taste like molasses.

Holoholona ✦ Animals

Although the wild and domesticated animal life of Niihau is not extensive, it helps to influence the lifestyle of islanders. Native Niihau *manu*, or birds, include duck, plover, turnstone curlew and similar species. Imported birds to be found on Niihau include pheasant, California quail, prairie chicken, mynah, several species of partridge and the western lark. Many birds migrate from the outer islands to Niihau, especially from the islands of Nihoa and Lehua.

The *holo holona* or introduced animals on Niihau used for domestic purposes include chickens, Merino sheep, short-horn cattle, Arabian horses, peacocks, wild turkeys and pigs. There once were dogs, cats and goats on the island. All dogs were ordered killed when the island became ranch land, as they were considered a threat to the sheep. Goats were eradicated by Lester Robinson because they competed with other livestock for pasture. Wild cats were also exterminated.

Puaa or pig hunting is done by roping or simply chasing the pig on horseback until it turns. Then the cowboy grabs the pig and ties him to a tree to await slaughter. Or he'll grab the pig's ears and finish him off with a knife on the spot. If in the course of daily work a cowboy comes across a pig, he is allowed to stop work and kill it.

There once were thousands of *pokeokeo*, or turkeys, on Niihau. As recently as the 1940s and 1950s, the turkeys were corralled, placed on wagons and brought to headquarters for fattening and then taken to market. They fattened the turkey with ground *kiawe* beans and cactus leaves. Since the outside market has become too competitive, the export of turkeys has been discontinued. However, *hipa*, or sheep ranching, is still an island industry. Sheep are sheared at Nonopapa, where the wool is graded, sorted and put in sacks for shipment to the mainland markets. Shearing is done with electric shears powered by a generator. Wool is sometimes stained by the red dirt on the island, making it difficult to sell. Sheep are also sold to other ranches, or sold for meat off-island.

The *pikake* or peacocks were introduced to Niihau around 1860. In the old days, the women used to make beautiful hat leis from the *pikake* feathers. Today, the serenity of Niihau is constantly disrupted by the screaming birds.

Lawaia ✦ Fishing

The people of Niihau have always relied on the sustenance provided by the ocean—*lawaia*, or fishing, is a necessity and as well a recreation. Fish abound in the clear waters of Niihau, as do other seafoods. Niihauans are choosy about the type of fish they eat. They practice the art of conservation by fishing only certain types of fish seasonally. Some favorite fish are *popolo, moi, ahole, nenue, kala* and *manini*. *Opihi* are plentiful and grow in the shallow waters on the *papa*. It is easy to harvest them. Just kick them off the reef. Niihau has one of the finest fishing grounds in Kauai County. Although islanders are not in possession of sophisticated fishing gear, the permanent shoal of plentiful fish that surrounds Niihau has always been for residents only and *kapu* to others. This restricted fishing area reaches from the outer reefs to the sands of the island. This law, decreed by Kamehameha III in 1839, has been rigorously enforced by the residents of Niihau. There is never a need for them to travel to other islands for food.

The fish that are caught and consumed on Niihau are frequently caught in special fishing areas, or *koa*, usually very deep holes on the bottom of the ocean. Niihauans had varied *koa* where they would fish for *moi*, or threadfish. Kawaihoa and Keanahaki Bay each contain a *moi koa*. Others were near the islands of Lehua and Kaula.

There are many Hawaiian sayings associated with the skill of fishing:

Nee kulo aka lawaia ua ma malie — "When the fisherman crouches low it is calm." This would signal that it is time to fish on the reef or at shore.

Kahi e no ka malie hoomakaukau ka makau — "The calm is far off, make ready the fishhooks." There might be rough waters now, but don't wait for the calm. Be ready beforehand.

Kau ka iwa, he la makani — "When the frigate bird flies, it will be a windy day."

Au ka toae, he la malie — "When the *koae* swims, it is a calm day." A good day for fishing.

Na Ia Ono o Ka Aina
The Savored Fish of the Land

Na keiki lawaia o ka aina *ahe kama eu no na kiu eiwa.*	The fisherman of the land, the child of the nine *kiu* winds.
O ke AHOLE lae o ka Hololoa *hei ana ika upena a ka lawaia.*	The spotted *ahole* of Hololoa, gilled in the net of the fisherman.
Aloha ka MANINI maka POPOLO *he mau ia noho ia i ka lau laupapa.*	Cherished is the *manini* and *popolo*, the fish that lives in the leaves of the reef.
O ke KALA ka NENUE o ka naha *wele moani keala ke honio aku.*	The *kala* and *nenue* of the seaweed, fragrant to the pallet to behold.
He ala LIPOA ua kaulana *he ono laulii no ka ehu kai.*	Famous is the fragrance of the *lipoa*, savory little leaves of the ocean spray.
O ka papa kaulana ao PAHEE *o ke AHOLE WAI piko lihaliha.*	The famous reef of Pahee with the rich *piko* of the Aholewai.
He moani ai a kou kopuu *me ka POI UWALA hanahana pono.*	The aroma that stimulates your taste buds, accompanied by the *uwala poi* . . . delicious.
Oka maka makolu ka upena ia *hei na ia o ke kai lipo lipo.*	The three fingered mesh, that's the net.
Ua lawa na ono a KAHELELANI *me ka like kahi kolu kiekie loa.*	Content is Kahelelani, physically and spiritually from the heavens above.
He ola no wau i ka MAKUA LANI *meka like kahi kolu kiekie loa.*	My life comes from God above, the father, the son and the holy ghost.
Haina ka inoa ua lohe ia *na ia kaulana o ka aina.*	These are the names that have been heard of the famous fish of this land.
Haina hou ia mai hana kapuana *na ia ono o ke kai lipo lipo.*	My story has been told again of the tasty fish of the dark blue seas.

Co-composer: Keola Kauiolehua Keamoai.
(Parts of this song recorded under "Aloha ka Manini")

Hee ✦ Octopus

Octopus fishing was commonly done on all of the islands, but the historic use of olivine and cowry shell for lure was peculiar to Niihau. In 1892, H. Bolton described the lure in *Some Hawaiian Pastimes:*

On Niihau, they fished for octopus with two strong hooks (formerly made of bone) attached to a line weighted in a fashion peculiar to the island. The hooks were fastened between a spotted cowry shell (*Cypraea*) and a hemispherical mass of olivine. Olivine is a common constituent of certain lavas and it is a very brilliant green. The stones were about the size of a half orange. This olivine was sought by the men of Niihau on the Island of Kaula. The Niihauans believed that the shell and the brilliant green stone attracted the octopus. Certain specimens of the stone were very highly treasured. They also had a belief that the stones lost their *mana* if one cooked a octopus that was caught with the lure. Sometimes men would steal a little piece of another's octopus and cook it, thus destroying the *mana* of the other's lure.

The Niihauans today eat octopus raw, cooked and also dried.

Mullet Farming

Another popular method of fishing is the continued practice of mullet farming. All of the mullet on Niihau are fat. When they are cleaned for eating, it is difficult to find the intestines. The mullet do not taste of mud and are highly marketable and very excellent in taste. Niihau mullet are frequently caught as *pua*, or babies, packed in barrels and transported alive to lakes and mullet ponds. When grown, they are marketed on Kauai and Oahu. Other *pua* swim from the ocean through a lava tube tunnel to Lake Halulu. The mullet are raised there and grow up to be of a good size, some of them eight to nine pounds apiece. A *kapu* from the times of old governed the mullet in Lake Halulu. The old saying goes, "If one scale from any fish there falls, all the fish in the lake will die." The reasoning behind this is that if somebody catches fish in Lake Halulu, everyone in Niihau should have a share. If it is time to harvest the fish, all the people of Niihau go and catch the fish and everyone shares in the catch.

Today, people have gone in with throw nets and within days of fishing, there will be dead mullet all over Lake Halulu. Nobody can hide the transgression of fishing. It still happens today. Also to this day, ocean water comes through the tunnel.

There are other mullet ponds on Niihau. There is a landlocked lake called Halalii, which is twice the size of Lake Halulu. However, Halalii is not really considered a lake; it is rather a low, salty, flat area. In time of heavy rain, it becomes large and five to six feet deep. When summer comes, the water recedes and becomes warm and the fish die. The mullet are put there by the work crews that go to the seashore and catch the small fry. They put them in barrels and transport them by truck to Lake Halalii, where they are released. They grow until the waters recede, then they are caught and sent to Kauai and Oahu markets by barge. Some are given to the people of the island. The fish grow to approximately three to four pounds.

Another old mullet pond is located in the Kaununui area. This is a low-lying area where the ocean comes inland to form the lake. The fish swim up from the ocean to the lake. In recent times, the Robinsons dammed another place close to Kaununui, stocked mullet there and harvested them for market. The mullet are nine to ten pounds apiece. Kalanei is an area which is also in a low-lying place close to the beach. Mullet are stocked here and grow up to ten pounds.

Other Marine Animals

Other marine species on Niihau are the *oopu*, or goby fish, and *opae*, shrimp. The island has two types of *oopu*, one of which—the *paoo*—spawns in the ocean and is caught at Kaununui. The other lives and spawns in the mud high up in the mountain streams, where it hibernates for up to three years. The *oopu* and the shrimp are the same type as those found on Maui and were introduced early in the 1800s.

Small *opae* use the tunnel at Lake Halulu. At certain times of the year, red *opae* from the tunnel come out into the ocean by the thousands. Also at times you can see the red *opae* in Lake Halulu. The old Niihau ladies used to go down to the lake and catch *opae* to bring home to eat. However, if before they entered the water the first person to see the *opae* would gasp in amazement *"auwe"* or "ayeee," the *opae* would disappear. Fact or legend, the people say it continues to happen to this day.

Small fresh water shrimp, similar to those in the mountain streams, are called *opae kalaole*. The only difference is that the *opae* are red in color.

Tohola or whales come to Niihau regularly, usually during the spawning season of the *manini*, when they feed upon the young fish. The Hawaiian monk seal or *ilio holo ika uaua* is common on the shores of Niihau and Lehua, where they lay on the reef sunbathing. They range from large adults to babies and are gray or black, and sometimes spotted. Children can walk right up to these seals without fear.

The relationship between the people of Niihau, their island and the sea is a simple balance of need, respect and dependency. It illustrates the beauty of the human spirit when it is in harmony with the natural resources that give life. This dependency is the foundation of Niihauans' love for the creatures with whom they share their land and ocean.

Niihau fishermen and canoes. (*Photo: Auckland Institute & Museum*)

CHAPTER VI

Myths & Legends of Heros & Demigods

*E ola kakou a mau loa
akau i ke ao malamalama*

May we live long until we ride the clouds of heaven

Keanaoku, the cave of Kuhaimoana, the shark guardian, Kaula. (*Photo: Bishop Museum*)

STORYTELLING ON NIIHAU was an important art—not only are tales a way to communicate heritage, spiritual faith and respect, but they are an entertainment that arouses the imagination. The following tales are but a small sampling of the stories that would fill the quiet Niihau evening.

Elima Kumu Ulu
Five Breadfruit Trees

Legend tells of five beautiful female *kupua* who came to Niihau from Tahiti. Their names were Hikinaakala, Kulimoku, Hakaleleaponi, Kalama and Nauluhuaikahapapa. As was the custom of all people from Tahiti who ventured to new lands, these *kupua* could not stay long in Hawaii—they were required to return to Tahiti before the sun rose, or at least to hide during the daylight hours. But these girls were having such a grand time frolicking on the southern part of the isle that they failed to notice that dawn was breaking. The sun rose, and the penalty for their disobedience was harsh: they were all turned into *ulu*, or breadfruit trees. Only these five *ulu* trees have grown on Niihau; no others have ever been planted or grown. Tutu Kaui said that one of the trees bled blood-red sap when cut or damaged; she was called Kulimoku. Only one of these trees remain today—Nauluhuaikahapapa.

Pupulenalena
The Kupua Dog of Niihau

Pupulenalena was a very famous dog of Niihau. He was a *kupua,* one who could change his body form at will. He roamed the islands doing very mischievous things, and he especially loved to steal. The following story was told to Tutu Kauai in 1930 when he left Niihau to go to Waimea, Kauai, to work as a cowboy for the Gay and Robinson plantation. The story was told to him by Kuwalu, a man who lived to be 104 years old.

While on Niihau, Pupulenalena had heard that the pig god Kamapuaa had planted a very beautiful garden at Makana in Haena, Kauai. The garden had a very sweet-smelling *hinahina* and a very fragrant *lauae* that smelled like the sweet *maile* vine. Mischievous as he was, Pupulenalena decided he was going to Kauai to steal some of the plants and bring them back to Niihau.

He knew that this would infuriate Kamapuaa, so with much speed, he went to Kauai. He climbed to the top of the mountain and as he reached the top, the air was filled with the sweet smell of the plants. In haste, he dug up as much *hinahina* as he needed. As he started digging up the *lauae*, he spotted the pig god Kamapuaa coming up the mountain in a rage to defend his garden from intruders.

Pupulenalena knew Kamapuaa had seen him so he ran down the mountain to Waiokapalae, the wet cave, where he dove into the water and disappeared. Upon entering the water, he changed into his crab form, called *papaipaakea*, which is very hard to see in the water as it looks very much like *limu*, or seaweed. Pupulenalena reached the beach at Haena and swam for home.

In the meantime, Kamapuaa had reached the wet cave. He didn't see the dog but he did see its tracks leading into the water, so he dove in the water, changing himself into his fish form called *humuhumunukunukuapuaa*, so as to make better time to catch the thief that raided his garden. When he reached the beach, no one was there so on to Niihau he went.

By then, Pupulenalena had already climbed the Kaali cliffs and planted the first *lauae* and *hinahina* at Kaalipuaa. Kamapuaa, in hot pursuit and still raging mad, spotted Pupulenalena up on the cliffs and gave chase along the mountain range, passing Pueo and on to Paia, hoping to catch up. But Pupulenalena was too fast and he was already resting at Kailioopapai in his crab form, watching Kamapuaa searching relentlessly.

After a while, Kamapuaa became thirsty because he had run so hard, so he paused for a drink in Honoula at the *punawai* called Waiakapuaa. While drinking and resting, he noted a reflection in the water: the dog hanging from the tree above his head, exposing his genitals. This area is named Kamailewalewa. By the time Kamapuaa came out of shock, Pupulenalena was long gone and was sunning himself on the reef at Kailioopapai. When he saw Kamapuaa he headed for Waaiu. In this area there are a lot of saltwater *loko*, or ponds.

Oh, how Pupulenalena loved being so playful! He was having a grand time teasing Kamapuaa and again he changed himself to a crab, escaping through an exit at the far end of the pond. He watched the pig god from the cave Keanaakekolo, the Cave Where You Crawl. After some time passed, Kamapuaa began to tire and he decided to rest at Mauuloa (long grass). While he was resting, he devised a plan to fool Pupulenalena. Kamapuaa knew that the dog was watching him from somewhere so he pretended to be farming. This area has a lot of *pili* grass. After he was sure the dog wasn't watching him, he piled the grass into bundles, tossed it over his shoulder and, disguising himself as an old man, went to Mauuhaawi.

Kamapuaa approached Pupulenalena at Haeakailio. The dog began to bark, and he continued to bark as the man came closer, not aware of who he really was. Coming close to the dog, Kamapuaa flung the bundles from his shoulder and lunged for Pupulenalena. At this point, the dog knew exactly who the man was and with the speed of lightning, took off and disappeared. Kamapuaa followed his tracks to Puuokama and Kaholeinapuaa, a *punawai*, where he stopped for a drink of water. (Today, the *punawai* is dry.) As Kamapuaa was drinking, he looked up and saw Pupulenalena at Kaununui on the beach at Kepuhi, moving north to Kawaiakailio.

Pupulenalena started digging under these rocks and found water. Here he changed himself into the crab and disappeared from Kamapuaa's view. He headed north to Puukole Point and entered the Halii Channel (between Lehua and Niihau) towards Lehua. This time Kamapuaa did not continue the chase, as he was distracted by another intruder and so he headed back to his garden on Kauai, thus ending the chase that encircled the entire island. Even today the *lauae* and *hinahina* that Pupulenalena stole still grow with their fragrant scents on the cliffs of Kaali.

Puulenalena is the real name of the dog. Somehow during his travels and different masters, his name was changed to Puapualenalena. A *hula* was written for him—the Hula Ilio—and it is considered a classic.

Koialaau and Koiauka
The Talking Stones

Koiauka and Koialaau were two *kupua*, or supernatural, stones that could talk. One night these two *kupua* turned themselves into human beings during one of their conversations. They were discussing where they wished to be for the rest of their lives.

Koiauka said that he did not wish to be close to the ocean, so he was going to place himself up on dry land. Koialaau said he would rather remain down close to the ocean—and so the teasing began.

> Koialaau: "If you go way up on dry land, the sun will shine on you and make you hot. The birds will mess all over you. The *moo*, or lizard, will crawl all over you and make you *kapulu*, dirty."
>
> Koiauka: "If you place yourself in the ocean, the *limu* will grow all over you, the *ina*, or sea urchin, will live in the cracks. The *puhi*, the eel, will crawl inside you and the ocean will put *lepo*, or dirt, all over you."

This conversation went on and on for quite a while. According to legend, because they were *kupua*, they could not let the rays of the sun shine on them, or they would be turned to stone. But they became so engrossed in their conversation that the first rays of the sun touched Koiauka and he was immediately turned into stone. Since he was upland, he remains there today in a grove of *kiawe* trees. Koialaau, upon seeing this happen, ran out of the water to help Koiauka, but he too was turned into stone. He was left on a cliff ledge where he stayed until the 1956 tidal wave. At that time, he was swept off the ledge into the ocean where he had wanted to be. The two of them may still be seen today.

When Kuhaimoana and Lanaikahiki Battled

Lanaikahiki was a Kaukaualii, a high class of chief, from the land of Tahiti who could change his *honu*, or turtle, body into any form—animal or human—at will. Lanaikahiki had decided to visit Niihau, but before going there he made the customary call at Kaula to see Kuhaimoana, the shark guardian of Niihau, who lived at Keanaoku.

Lanaikahiki swam into the cave and was greeted by Kuhaimoana. Lanaikahiki asked Kuhaimonana for permission to tour Niihau. After much deliberation, the shark god said, "Yes, I will grant you permission, but with one condition: that I accompany you on your tour and that you swim on your side of the ocean." By this Kuhaimoana meant that there are boundaries that divide the sea. Near Niihau is Kuhaimoana's domain, called Kaikapuoku, or the forbidden seas of Ku. Anything that fell into the ocean within this boundary would continue to live due to the efforts of the shark god. Anything that fell into the other side would surely be eaten.

As they swam side by side, they came to Kawahamana. As the two reached this area, Lanaikahiki noticed all the surfers and turned to Kuhaimoana and said he was hungry and would like to eat some crabs—meaning the surfers. Kuhaimoana reminded Lanaikahiki that he had asked permission only to sightsee and not to come and eat his people, but Lanaikahiki insisted, and with that, the two of them got into a terrible fight. Kuhaimoana took time out from the fight to use all the powers given him. He ordered a huge wave that took all the surfers onto shore and safety. As the fight continued, the two drifted toward the south side of the island to Kahae. Then Kuhaimoana started to push the *honu* towards the shallow water, but since he could not manage well in shallow water, he summoned the help of two small *halalu*. These small fish succeeded in beaching the *honu* on the rocks, where the rays of the sun touched the turtle and turned him into stone. There he remains to this very day.

Because he was pushed out of the water and floated, he was called Lana, and because he was from Kahiki, or Tahiti, his name was Lanaikahiki (Lana of Tahiti). The real name of the turtle was Luahiva. *Ku hohonu ka lua o Kuhaimoana* — "Deep indeed is the cave of Kuihaimoana" is now said of a prosperous person.

Puhiula
The Red Eel Guardian God of the Ocean

There are two versions of the story about Puhiula, the giant red eel that swam to an area close to Kamalino, on the southwestern side of Niihau. One tale comes from an old man named Nohokula; the other from Kalua Keale. This is Kalua Keale's version.

Two men from the island of Maui came to Niihau to fish. They were brothers and they were called Pahaunui and Pahauiki. The elder brother, Pahaunui, was always hungry, and in order to satisfy that hunger he had to have an eel. After spending the day fishing and filling up their sacks, the elder brother was very hungry and wished to have his eel. The younger brother knew that he would have to satisfy his brother or they would not get back to Maui. Out into the ocean went the two men to obtain more fish to make *hauna*, or chum, which would attract any eels in the area. For the rest of the day, they threw the *hauna* into the water but it seemed that none of the eels around Niihau would take the bait. Through the night they threw the *hauna* and as they continued, the *hauna* began to spread out into the waters past Kaula Rock, then on to Motu Papapa and to Tahiti. (Motu Papapa is on the other side of Kaula Rock towards the southwest from Niihau, halfway to the island of Tahiti, according to Tutu Kaui.) At this point, one eel was attracted to the smell and began to follow the scent to Niihau. The eel's name was Puhiula, a *kupua* from Tahiti. As he was coming toward Niihau, all the red fish in the ocean cleared his way. When Puhiula neared Niihau, the two men spotted him and became very excited and threw out more and more *hauna*. Puhiula took the bait and was captured!

As Pahaunui was bringing in the eel, he ordered his brother to ready the *imu*—so that when they landed the eel they could eat—then hurry back to help prepare this large eel. Puhiula was so large that the men had a hard struggle getting him out of the water. Finally, they managed to get the head and half of the body out of the water. At this point, one of the brothers got his stone axe and cut up the body. But each time they cut the body, it would rejoin. Time and time again, they tried to chop the body up but with no success.

Finally, Puhiula turned to the men and said, "Just cut off my head and throw it back into the water and then you will be able to eat my body." The brothers agreed to do this; they cut off the head. But they were very hungry, and rather then throwing the head into the ocean, they greedily put the head into the *imu* and cooked it. While the head was cooking, they cut the body into four equal sections. Hunger finally overpowered them, so they quickly ate the head. The head was so large and they soon were full—the two had eaten all except for the snout. Now that their *opu*, or stomachs, were full, they lay down for a rest. As morning approached, the first rays of sunlight fell on the brothers and Puhiula, turning them into stone, as they remain today. There, the stone body of the eel, minus the head, still lies halfway out of the water, chopped up into equal four foot sections. The *imu* remains still on the shore nearby. It is said that if the brothers had eaten the entire head, including the snout, they would not have been turned to stone.

Pilikua
The Giants

In the middle of the plain on the north end of the island, standing by itself, is a small round hill called Pakehoolua. This is the story behind that hill. Many hundred of years ago, there were giants that lived throughout the islands. One great giant lived on Kauai; another lived on Niihau. As was custom, they continually taunted and bragged to each other across the Kaulakahi Channel. Their booming voices shook the land when they were angry. One day while the two were teasing each other, anger arose. Each was trying to show the other that he was greater and had much more strength. They began to shout, "Men who eat sweet potato are strong. Men who eat *poi* are weak." Angered, they threw rocks at each other. The Niihau man's rock fell short of Kauai landing, just outside the breakers at Mana. It has a big white cross on it and is still seen today. The Kauai man tore off a piece of the *pali*, or cliff, behind Mana and hurled it on Niihau, killing the Niihau giant. His bones lie there today underneath the mound of Kauai dirt known as Pakehoolua. On each island there is a part of the other, and the boasts remain until today.

Three Aikanaka
The Tattooed Man-Eaters From the South

Niihau had three *aikanaka*, or man-eaters, who killed and ate anyone who might happen along. They would patrol and wait for the fishermen of Niihau and Kauai to pass by. A young chief from Kauai named Ola decided to end this. He took his canoe and left Kauai for Niihau. In order to fool the *aikanaka*, he carved four wooden men from *ohia* wood, which, when placed in his canoe, made it look like there were five people. As he neared Niihau, he lay low in the canoe so it appeared that there were only four men. The three *aikanaka* spotted the canoe with the four men, thinking that there was another good meal. They would wait until dark and then eat them. In the meantime, Ola had taken the four wooden *tiki* and placed mother-of-pearl into the eyes and then put them in a resting position in a *hale* he built. Ola hid in the *kiawe* bush to wait, for he knew he could kill these men with his magic club. Night fell and the three *aikanaka* arrived. They were astonished to see the four men sleeping with their eyes open but since they did not move, they must be sleeping. The man-eaters started eating the sleeping men, but because they were made of wood, they stuck in the cannibals' teeth. The *aikanaka* said, *"Paakiki na kanaka o Kauwai"* — hard are the men of Kauai. At this point, Ola came from behind and killed the *aikanaka*, fed them to the sharks and then returned to Kauai. The area Kii was named after the four wooden men.

The Sons of Haka and Their Flight to the Puuhonua

This is the story of Haka's two sons who found themselves in very serious trouble with pursuers. The two boys started running toward Kaunuapua, the *puuhonua*, but their pursuers got in between and cut them off from the place of refuge. The eldest boy—the fastest runner of the two—called out to his brother to head toward the mountain towards Kamalu. As the pursuers were closing in on the youngster, he called out for the elder brother to roll some boulders down on them while he ran clear. The rocks came hurtling down the side of the mountain, giving the younger brother time to catch up. The two boys crossed the mountain to the cliffs facing Kauai. The younger brother was so frightened of being captured that he told the elder brother he was going to jump off this *pali*. The elder embraced the younger and said, "If you jump off this *pali* our *aumakua*, the *pueo* or owl, might see you and save you, but if he does not, you will die."

The pursuers were closing in so the boy jumped! The *pueo* saw the boy, caught him mid-air, and stuffed him into a crevice on the side of the mountain. But the crevice was so small that his feet stuck out. The pursuers below saw his shaking legs and began to throw rocks. Later that night, with the elder brother standing on his wings, the *pueo* came to wake the younger one. All left for Keanapueo to hide until enough time passed so that they could safely return to the village. In the morning, the pursuers looked for the kicking legs and feet on the mountainside, but saw nothing so they gave up the search. A little later, the *pueo* took them out of the cave and returned them to the village. This is one of the stories told to Tutu Kaui by Kalua Keale in relation to the *puuhonua heiau*.

Halemanuahi
A Tale of He Lua

The following story about *lua*, or the art of self-defense, tells of a Niihau couple who lived at Halemanuahi, near the *punawai* Kalehua. One day the husband and his wife had started the usual preparations for the day's food. They gathered the sweet potatoes and fish and were about to put them into the *imu*. This was the husband's job, so he said to his wife, "You had better go to Kalehua *punawai* for some water while I stay here and watch the *imu*." Obediently the wife picked up her *huewai*, or water gourd, and started for the *punawai*. As she was filling the *huewai* with water, she was roughly seized from behind. The water gourd fell to the ground and she struggled for freedom, but to no avail. There were too many men, six to be exact.

She did not recognize these strangers, but these men were the dreaded *Mu* people from Kauai who searched Niihau for human sacrifices. They had landed their canoes on the east side of Niihau at Konouli, carrying the canoes ashore and hiding them in a grove of *wiliwili* trees. The grove of trees is still there today. After hiding the canoes, they climbed up the *pali*, or cliffs, then came over the mountain and down onto the flat area on the western side of the island, where they came upon the woman. As she tried to fight them off, she soon realized that it was to no avail. They overpowered her, tied her up and carried her off.

Meanwhile, her husband at home began wondering what was taking her so long to do such a simple task. So the husband went looking for her. As he approached Kalehua, he saw his wife's water gourd on the ground. He look around for her and saw the footprints and signs of a struggle. He followed the tracks to Keanakeina. As the man stood there, he caught sight of six men carrying his wife up the side of the mountain at Haulikule. Seeing his wife captive caused him to speed up his pursuit. The *Mu* people, being good hunters for the king of Kauai, also sighted the man in pursuit, so two of them stayed behind to fight him off. Unknown to the two, the husband was a *lua* expert. The two men leaped to attack him and before their bodies touched the ground, the husband removed their eyeballs and *akeloa*, or spleen, and tore them apart. He then continued onward.

As the husband came to Puulua, two more men stayed behind to do battle. When they came for him, he took care of them in the same fashion as the other two. He continued on up to the valley of Kaailana. Here, he finally closed the gap between himself and his enemies.

The last two men were close to the canoes by now, so they released the woman and turned to do battle. *Auwe!* They too were demolished by the *lua* expert in the same fashion as the others; however, this time the husband ate the eyeballs, *ake*, or liver, and *akeloa!*

It seems that the *lua* practitioners worshiped Kuialua, the god of Lua, and when the victor ate his victim's innards, they believed the victor was feeding Kuialua. After paying homage to his god of Lua, the husband, with a tear in his eye, tenderly picked up his wife and headed home. As they neared their *hale*, he saw a group of people at a distance advancing toward him. *Auwe*, he thought, Must I do battle again? But as they neared the crowd, they realized it was their own flesh and blood, the *ohana* who had come to find them. Much joy and many tears followed at the reunion. Together they all returned to the house where they all partook of the food that was cooked in the *imu*.

Kauanaulu Demonstrates His Skill at He Lua

Kauanaulu, the father of Moses Kaaneikawahaale Keale, was a remarkable man. At the age of 75, he was as straight and tall as he had been during his youth. Kauanaulu was well-known as an expert in the Hawaiian art of self-defense known as *he lua*. Many stories have been told of his strength and skill, even until today, and the following is but one of many.

While Kauanaulu was walking with some friends over the mountains from Kalalau to Waimea, he met a stranger coming down the path in the opposite direction near Halemanu. Kauanaulu invited the stranger to join them for a little food and conversation. Time came when Kauanaulu had to continue on over the mountains, so they parted from the stranger and started up the path. After a short while, one of Kauanaulu's friends looked back to see the stranger following. Kauanaulu, being the expert he was, did not look back—he knew this meant an attack—but instead told the friends to go on and he would follow. He started to walk a little slower so the stranger could catch up with him. As the stranger placed his hand on Kauanaulu, he threw the stranger over his shoulder, breaking his back and killing him instantly.

Even in his old age, Kauanaulu was tested by both young and old, but he retained his skill and quickness. Kauanaulu was also versed in the art of navigation. He passed on to his son Kapahee an exact and profound knowledge of the sea based on observation of earth movement, seasons, the stars and the peculiarities of all the winds. Each of these things was important. Trips on the open ocean were set in accordance with the rising and setting of the sun. The trips to and from Tahiti were during the spring and fall trade winds.

Kapahee Nui
The Navigator

Kapahee, a brother of Moses Kaaneikawahaale Keale and a son of Kauanaulu, was known for his feats of bravery. Like his brother, Kapahee lived at Kalalau, Kauai, where his family had large land holdings. Most of their crop was taro, and it was from these taro patches that Kapahee would take boat loads of the crop to Niihau for his relatives.

He was at home in the water, whether swimming fifteen miles or handling the whale boats. He was fearless. The Sinclairs hired him as head boatman to navigate the sometimes rough channel between Kauai and

Niihau. Kapahee was well-versed in the art of ocean navigation; he had been taught by his father. Together they made numerous trips to Tahiti and back. He also was credited with saving many people's lives, usually from overturned whale boats during rough seas, including Valdemar "Kanuka" Knudsen, whom he saved twice from the waters.

In 1893, Kapahee, who was now in his late sixties, boarded the steamer *Waialeale* bound for Honolulu and Kalaupapa, Molokai. It was to be his last boat trip. He was one of the lepers taken from Kalalau Valley and by then, his face was badly infected with leprosy. He died and was buried on Molokai. Kapahee's sister, Lepekakakailianu, was a very tall and strong woman who has been credited with several water rescues.

CHAPTER VII

Place Names of Niihau

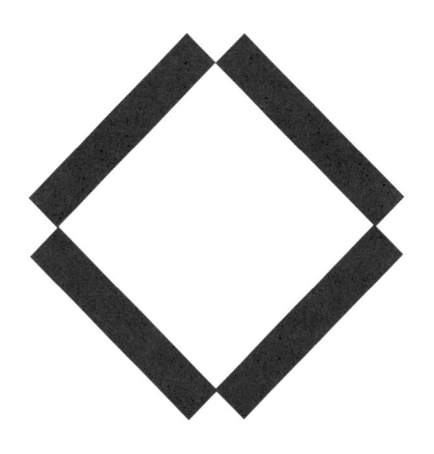

*Ohia nalu kaulana
pula kau maka a na kupuna*

Famous are the waves of Ohia that
splashed in the eyes of our ancestors

Northern end of Niihau's central plateau, 1928. (*Photo: Bishop Museum*)

Place Names of Niihau

To THE KAMAAINA of Niihau, nearly every rock, cove, beach, mountain, valley and spring has a name and a story. Below is a fine example of an older composition that uses place names and geographical or natural descriptions to preserve the places in memory. These names were known by a few old timers and, for the most part, have been recorded in Niihau ledgers. These names, however, have never been published—maps of the island do not record them. They live in the legends and *mele*, and the everyday lore of the people.

Mele ✦ Traditional Song

Kaali wai mapuna
hoopulu ka liko lau hinahina.

Water from Kaali moistens
the leaf of the *hinahina*.

Noho ana o Kanalo ika ulu wehi
lau oka nui ani ka makani.

There is Kanalo, with the leaf
of the coconut that sways in the wind.

Puhueloa ake kula loa
hooheno ia nei me Puu o Hawaii.

Puheloa is a flat plain
close to Puuwai.

Keoneloaohaena
a hai loa malu ke kiawe.

The sands of Haenaloa
are shaded by the *kiawe*.

Ka piina o Kalihilihi ea
kaluna kapu a o Maunaleo.

The incline of Kalihilihi
is the only way to sacred Maunaaleo.

Kaununui heiau kapu
noho ana ika poli o Kauwaha.

Kaununui possesses a sacred place,
Kauwaha, which it cradles in its breast.

Kaaiea kuli koolau
hooheno ika luna o Halealii.

Kaaiea faces the koolau
close to the top of Halealii.

Ohia nalu kaulana
pula kau maka a na kupuna.

Famous are the waves of Ohia
that splashed in the eyes of our ancestors.

Pukaiti wai mapuna
aina ike kula maniania.

The water from Pukaiki
lies in a flat meadow.

Haaheo na wai ekolu
Keaona, Waihuna ame Waiui.

Famous are the three waters
of Keaona, Waihuna and Waiui.

Iubile malu ike kiawe
kuu home laa ia kuu hoomana.

Iubile shaded by kiawe,
my sacred place, my religion.

Puuwai kau mai iluna *hooheno ia mai e ka Naulu.*	Looking up to Puuwai caressed by the Naulu wind
Waiaka hani i ka makani *na kiu eiwa koni ika ili.*	Waiaka flirts with the winds, the nine cold winds that tingle the skin.
Haina ia mai hana kapuana *kamakua lani kou alakai.*	This ends my song, my father in heaven is my guide.
Haina hou ia mai hana kapuana *Ekolu no pua lawa kuu lei.*	My story is told, The three flowers, my lei is done.

By Moses Wehekealakaluaikahakaaulana Keale.
Circa 1896.

Na Wahi Pana ✦ General Place Names

The beauty of the Hawaiian language is revealed in the many literal, figurative and spiritual meanings given to island sites and features. Only a people who understood the nuances and power of their island home could have so masterfully given these places their names. The following are interesting histories and legends associated with place names of general interest.

Haleopaweo. This is the house foundation site of Moses W. Kaaneikawahaale Keale, one of the founders of the Iubile Church, and the founder of Hoomana Ia Iesu.

Kaiwimoeonakupuna (The Sleeping Bones of Our *Kupuna*). Near the town of Puuwai at Halehaa is the place called Kaiwimoeonakupuna. There are actually no bones here, only the long and pointed land-snail shells. These shells are found inland in the dry sand dunes. It is said if one was to go and dig in the dunes, one would find not just a single shell, but many of them, and surprisingly the snails inside would still be alive. This is why the name is Kaiwimoeonakupuna. The shell is actually called Pupumoeone.

Kaluakahua. It is said that these sand dunes sing. The Niihauans say that the sounds from the shifting sands are caused by the *uhane*—the spirits—of the dead that are buried there. They moan because they are disturbed. There are still well-preserved skeletons in evidence.

In 1892, George S. Gay had a guest on Niihau who took a skull from the dunes. Climbing aboard the whaleboat bound for Kauai, Mr. Gay was told of this "treasure." Mr. Gay warned the *haole* not to let the boatmen see it, as they were very superstitious and would refuse to start the voyage. The day they left Niihau, it was clear and calm. The trip to Waimea, Kauai, from the Kii landing on Niihau usually takes four to six hours, but for some unknown reason, strong head winds, then no winds, then strong tides and heavy seas worked against the boat. The men rowed hard, but it took them over thirteen weary hours to cross. The man who had in his possession the skull now regards the superstitions of the Hawaiians as well-founded.

Kaluaakona. This was the home site of one of the old-timers, a *kupuna*, who lived at the time of Keale. His name was Kaimi. A stone wall still stands where his home was.

Kapapakiikii. This area was the *milu*, or the casting off place of the souls, also called Kaleinaakauhane. Kapapakiikii, Mauloku and Kahikiikalewa all relate to the dead in ancient times.

Kauanaulu. This was the original name of the town now called Puuwai; also the name of a man well-known in the art of *he lua* (Hawaiian art of self-defense). There is a saying for this area: "*Kau ke ao, Naulu, ola ka aina*" — "Aloft is the Naulu cloud, bringing life to the land."

Kaumuhonu. Named after a great chief and older brother of Chief Moikeha, both descendants from the Ulu lineage of Tahiti.

Kaunu. This is another name for Niihau in the language of the priests.

Keananoio. The northern end of Niihau has much evidence of an old fishing village. There were many *noio* birds who would act as spotters of the *moi* fish. This told the fishermen that great schools of *aku*, or skipjack, were nearby. This bird lives on fish and is found in colonies along the northern coast caves and ledges.

Kii. A landing location that was named for a demigod from the south.

Kuakealii (Canoe from Tahiti). Kuakealii had to be a canoe of the *alii*, since all legends passed from generation to generation say that the people who came to Niihau from Tahiti were *kaukaualii*, or of the *alii* class. This story is about a group of rocks situated near the area of Leahi. Supposedly, these Tahitians frequently came solely for recreation. They chose the Keanahaki cave at Kawaihoa for their spot. The legend says that these men received warnings from their *tupuna* (*kupuna*) to "go and enjoy yourselves but don't forget to come home before dawn." The men were having such a grand time that they didn't notice that dawn was about to break. When they did finally notice, they also remembered the warning and, in a last effort, raced for their canoe. *Auwe!* Too late! The rays of the sun beat down on them and turned them and their canoe into stone. Their canoe of stone can be seen today in the waters of Niihau. Next to the canoe is Na Koa, a group of stones that resembles the men who tried to get back before the sun turned them to stone. The men are all standing in a single file.

Lanakila. This is the site of Keale's church that was once at Kamalino. Actually, the name Kamalino is for a small *pukoo*, or rock, and is not the district where Lanakila or Paweo are situated. Tutu Kaui said the only reason people call the whole area Kamalino is because they don't know the actual specific names of the different places—each area has its own name and Kamalino is only a small place there.

Makalii. Named for the King of Niihau and Chief of Waimea, Kauai, who was father-in-law of Manokalanipo. A month and season are named after him. He spent much time on Niihau.

Niihau iki. This area, close to Kawaiaina, has a concrete place for a landing where the people of the island spend time sitting, sometimes fishing. There is a saying that visitors to Niihau go sightseeing all over the island, but only the *kamaaina* sit here at Niihau iki.

Pa Pohaku (Stone Wall). Across the entire lower quarter of Niihau, from Oiamoi to Makahauena, stands an ancient stone boundary wall, six to eight feet in height. *Olelo kahiko*, or tradition, says it divided two districts.

Puu Kaeo. This mountain was named after King Kaeokulani, King of Niihau and Chief of Kauai in the 1700s.

Puu o Hawaii. This is a small hill, special to the people of Niihau, reserved for *ohana*, or family, and rarely showed to visitors. On the side of this same hill was an old *punawai* with good, sweet, drinkable water. In those days, water was life to Niihauans. It was always cared for. Mud was taken out and care was taken that animals would not pollute the water. As time went by, however, they began to neglect the well, and *kiawe* trees sprouted and grew. The roots of the trees probably caused the lime rock below to crack and saltwater started seeping in, thus the *punawai* is now salty and of no use to the people.

Puu Paniau. The highest point on Niihau, Puu Paniau is 1,281 feet above sea level. Nearby, at Nanaikauwai, is where the islanders used to signal for help to Kauai, once with fire and in modern times with flashlights. Paniau is on the northern end of the island, toward the eastern shore. A ridge of mountains runs down the island's eastern side from north to south between these two points.

Tahiti Moe and **Piokeanuenue.** To the right of Nonopapa landing is an oblong rock known as Tahiti Moe. Looking down into the ocean, one will see a large crevasse. This is the passage that this rock used to reach land. Many of the elders had very strong beliefs in a "lost continent" homeland, and to them this stone was, in fact, from the homeland. As late as 1923, some of these Hawaiians observed an ancient custom of their forefathers in the offering to Tahiti Moe of *awa* and other foods. This was not necessarily a religious belief, only a custom. Nearby is a land cave, Keanakoko.

Also in this area, just above the water's surface as one looks seaward at dusk, when the tide starts to recede, is the brilliant red stone, *pohaku ula*, known as Piokeanuenue. Its story has been forgotten, but the stone has a very brilliant coloring.

Place Names of Niihau **VII**

Tipapa (Stone Road). There is a stone road that lies to the south of Kamalino. It runs on the shoreline at the high-water mark. This area has no sand at all but a lot of loose boulders and volcanic rock. The people of Niihau call it Tipapa, a stone path that was built in ancient times. It is about four feet wide and constructed of big, flat boulders. You can drive a jeep along it. Some of the rocks have been washed away by tidal-wave action, but it is still passable.

One elderly Niihau woman says she remembers some talk from her grandparents of this being a very sacred place, but she doesn't know the story behind it. Also above Tipapa are numerous stones stacked together with many others scattered about. This might have been a very large, old *heiau*, or temple, with several buildings in the compound, since the place names indicate the same: Kealoonakii, "the presence of our images," and Opuonakii, "the resting place of our images."

Awaawa ✦ Valleys

The following are Niihau's valleys, starting at Kalaeopueo, south to Paia, west to Kanaha Valley, north to the Kaali Cliffs, east to Poleho and south back to Kalaeopueo. (See map.)

Konouli	Kanaha	Mokouia
Kaailana	Apana	Kaali Cliffs
Awaawalua	Haao	Koolaukani
Nomilu	Kaumuhonu	Pakilehua (upper valley)
Hanakamanene	Keanaouhi	Kiialaka
Kalaoa	Kahunalii	Kamalukii (upper valley)
Waiakapuaa	Pohueloa	Puniakapo (upper valley)
Kalaalau	Kaaliali Nui	Kaailana
Honoaula	Kanalo	Puulua
Popolo Nui	Kanaloki	Honoulii

Keanaouhi is the largest valley. It is 600 feet deep near the mouth and almost one mile rim to rim.

Mele no na Pali
Chant of the Valleys

1 *Ui lani wale ai oka hoolapa*
   Me pueo i ka pali Kalahale.

2 *Na hale ekolu kau mai iluna*
   Me Konouli i kala laelae.

3 *Eia kaponiponi ike alo pali*
   Ike ala nihinihi kau e kaweli.

4 *Kaulana o Waiahuli*
   I ka noho i ka poli o Kaailana.

5 *A lawa ae oe ani kamakani*
   Haaheo ika luna o ka pikapi.

6 *Na Awaawalua e lua ia*
   Me ka pua kapu o ka pukapuka.

88 NIIHAU: The Traditions of a Hawaiian Island

7 He alii Nomilu no na kona
   Me ka paepae kapu o liloa.
8 Alo ana o kalae ika ehu kai
   Me Kapaleilei ua lei ia.
9 I ka lei ake ao ai malu ai
   Me Hanakamanene he ui mai hoi kau.
10 Kapuai o ale eha ale nei
   Me ka paina kakahiaka.
11 Healoha Kalaoa ika wehiwehi
   Me elieli na aka paa paaponoia.
12 Ua lino hau ia na kuahiwi
   Ika ohu haaheo ai Puulua.
13 Na kiu umuhana kupanaha
   Kapa lei hulu manu hulumelemele.
14 Healoha Kaeo lei naulu
   Ke kuvini kaulana o Kahelelani.
15 Kuina a Kahekili ika oleole
   Me na hai elua i Honoalua.
16 Oihana ia ua hana ia
   Me kalae kilo ia i Waiapuaa.
17 Kua mai Kaula elua ia
   Noho ana noho lua ika lau pali.
18 Aohe ou loa eluna Kahili
   Ika noho ika ehuehu o ke kai.

19 Eia o paia ika ulu wehi
   Me puili lima ia meke aloha.
20 Noho noho apola ika mapuna
   Me Puuhale lua ika laalaau.
21 Puainako ua hooko ia
   Me keala o kahiti o na kupuna.
22 Na Kialaa ika ulu nahele
   Me Popolonui ia kinamaka.
23 O ka maka kaulana ana kupuna
   No ke alielie o Kawainui.
24 O Halalii ike ko kaulana
   Me ka hanu ona ihu honi hoomau.
25 He kuono Wailana noho ika lulu
   Me keana a paa i pa huli honu.
26 O ka unu a kala ai Waiu
   Noho ana ina hale aka ohai.
27 Ua lawa kuulei ua lei ia
   Hoa hele o ka ua me kamakani.
28 He kupa mai au no Kahelelani
   Milimili na ka la welo i Lehua.
29 Haina ia hana kapuana
   Ekolu no pua lawa kuulei.

*This mele was written by Kalua Keale, circa 1890.
Translation unavailable.*

Kahakai Ame Awa Pae ✦ Beaches & Landings

The following stories and legends concern beach names and landings.

Kaaukuu (Keawa kau a Kaniela). This is a place where the supply boats land. However, if the water is too rough, then they land at Kii landing. The true name for Kaaukuu is Keawa kau a Kaniela.

Kaholonakauupena. This sandy beach was used as a navigational guide for fishermen who traveled out into the open ocean, or who had gone to Kaula Island to fetch some birds. This was the homing landmark for them. If they could not see the white sands of this beach, they were still out in the seas of Kaula. If they could spot the white sands, they knew they were safely back in the waters of Niihau.

Kahonupilau (Smelly Turtle). This place is named for a turtle that was washed up on the beach and stranded. He started to smell so badly the people thought that he was dead and were going to get rid of him. But he was still alive—thus the name.

Kailioopapai (The Dog Who Changed Himself into a Crab). This name refers to the legend of the *kupua* dog, Pupulenelena, at the time when he was on Niihau and changed himself into a crab. The Niihauans called this crab *papaipaakea*.

Kalaniwai, Kalanihale, Kaununaohiki. The original name for this area is Kalaniwai and it was used by the Robinsons as a boat landing. The Robinsons built a small house there and the name was changed to Kalanihale. Kalaniwai is the name of the *punawai* there. Kaununaohiki was a *heiau*.

Kaluaapuhi (The Hole of the Eel). This fishing *lua*, or hole, was so named because if the fishermen were not fast enough in retrieving their throw nets from it, eels would come and quickly steal the fish.

Kaumuhonu (The Oven of the Turtle). Legend has it that the people caught a *honu*, or turtle, dug an *imu*, put the *honu* inside, covered him and prepared for a feast. They did not know that the turtle was a *kupua*. After he was covered with dirt, he called a large wave to flood the *imu*, and escaped by digging his way out through a tunnel below.

Kapuaiokana (Footprint of Kana). Kana was a *kupua*, the brother of Niheu. According to legend, Kana was a giant who could step from one island to another, although they were miles apart. The story has been forgotten, but his footprint remains on Niihau. The left footprint of Kana is located next to Kaumuhonu. According to the residents there, the left print is on Niihau and the right footprint is on Mount Haupu on Kauai.

Kahalauwaa (House of the Canoes). This is a flat area where the ancient ones beached their canoes while in the area of Keanapou.

Kapena Kuke (Captain Cook). This place is named for Captain James Cook. The Niihau people insist that Niihau was the first place that Captain Cook landed, rather than at Waimea on Kauai! They say that if Waimea was the first place he landed, then why isn't it named after Captain Cook? There is a stone that has lines on it. The people of Niihau were fascinated with Captain Cook, so they scratched lines on the rock to measure the height of his jawline and the top of his head.

Kaunuakane (Altar of Kane). There are several ledges at different levels or a stairway on the side of this cliff that were later used to spot schools of fish. The *kilo*, or fish spotters, would sit up on these ledges and act as guides for the fishermen out in the canoes. They would lead them to the schools of fish.

Kaununui. This is one of the summer landing areas where the Robinsons' supply ships come in. As you stand at Kaununui facing the ocean and Nihoa, on the right side there is a big, flat reef that extends far out into the ocean. This beautiful *papa* is a favorite of the people for net throwing, for *ahole* and *nenue*.

Keanahio. A woman lived near Kamauuloa, in a place called Kamakaukeiki. One day she and her dog went down to the beach to pick some *opihi* at Keolapaakea. She had been picking *opihi* for only a short time and was so engrossed in what she was doing that she did not notice a canoe silently approaching from the open ocean. Her little dog saw the canoe and started barking. The woman paid no attention and kept on picking her *opihi*. The little dog barked again and then tugged at her clothing, trying to pull her toward the shore. Finally, the woman looked up and saw the canoe. She watched the canoeists awhile and then recognized the four men. They were the dreaded *Mu* people from Kauai! In the olden days, the *Mu* people came from Kauai to Niihau looking for human sacrifices. The woman, realizing what they were up to, ran towards a cave, Keanahio, with her little dog following. (It is not known for sure, but it is believed that in the old days, people prepared secret hiding places in certain parts of the island.)

The four *Mu* men landed their canoe. They pursued the woman and they felt very certain they would catch her. They followed her footprints in the sand and when they came to rocky areas, they could still follow her wet footprints into the cave. The men entered the cave, but to their astonishment, the footprints disappeared! They searched every corner of the cave and the sand beach on the other side of the cave, but still found nothing. They agreed that this woman must have been a *kupua* to have just disappeared like that, so they launched their canoe and continued around the island to find other sacrifices.

There was a secret hiding chamber in the roof of the cave, a large upper chamber into which one could climb. There was also a very large boulder to block the opening. The woman and her little dog had climbed into the upper chamber and sealed themselves from view by placing the large boulder over the roof opening. Thus they were saved from the terrible *Mu*.

The *Mu* people continued on their journey around the island in search of human sacrifices, eventually arriving at Keanahaki. Here they spotted an old couple working in their sweet potato field. The old people were also preparing an *imu* to cook some food when these strangers approached. The wife was the first to notice the canoe arriving. She told her husband, "There is a canoe coming." The old man looked at the canoe and then quietly told his wife to go to the *mauka* side of the *imu* while he took his place on the beach side of the *imu*. The couple acted as if nothing were wrong, continuing their work, paying no attention to the strangers. The *Mu* men talked among themselves, saying that one of them should grab the old man while the others should get the woman. As one of the *Mu* grabbed him, the old man quickly flipped the attacker into the *imu*, breaking the man's back while at the same time digging out his eyeballs. This is what the well-trained fighters of *lua* normally did.

The other three *Mu*, seeing what had happened, took off as fast as they could, running toward Kaumuhonu. After staying there a while, they came back to try and retrieve the canoe. As they neared the old folks, the old people called out to them, "Come, come, the *imu* is full and there is plenty for all of us." The three men approached cautiously, as they didn't know if the old man would do the same thing to them. After a while, they in fact accepted the invitation to eat with the old ones. While eating, the *Mu* men told of how the *alii* of Kauai had sent them to Niihau to fetch human sacrifices and they were very afraid as they had no one to bring back with them. The wise old man told them to take the one whose back he had broken. This they did, and thus the old man and his wife were spared.

Keanapou (Cave of Hangers or Posts). The entrance to this cave has no beach where canoes can be landed. In ancient times, the people sailed the canoes into the cave and suspended them from hangers or hooks in the ceiling of the cave. The ceiling hangers are still visible today.

Keikiakamanawa. This is a long, black rock out in the ocean. It is actually two rocks that are side by side. One faces the shore; the other looks out to sea. As legend has it, two children were stillborn and turned to stone. The Niihau people call it *poo wawae*, or head to toe, because of the different directions in which they faced. Tutu Kaui remarked that he himself swam around these rocks and they really appeared to be human, but they are indeed of stone.

Kie Kie. Long ago, this was where a woman had her home. The road passed right next to it. Now there is a gate there, *Pukapa*. The people from Puuwai or Kamalino had to pass this particular home on their way to or from the end of the island. In order to get permission to pass, each man had to sleep with the woman first, after which he was free to pass. It is not known what the results would be if passing men were to disobey her.

Kii. Long ago a visitor came to Niihau. She was an *alii* related to Pele and her name was Kapo. Kapo and friends danced a type of dance that resembled a *kii*. In her honor, the *alii* named the place after the dance. Another version of this place name is in a story called "Three Aikanaka," related in Chapter Six.

Konahina. In the old days, this was one of the places that the owners of the island considered for a supply boat landing. Most shore names on Niihau usually have a big rock, reef or outcropping for which they are named. Konahina is a large and flat rock with a sandy area. One of the problems they had in trying to make a landing out of this area was that while the sea may be calm inside the rock, there are big breakers outside, so this was not a good place for a landing. Konahina is located before Pakala.

Lonopapa. According to Tutu Kaui, this is where the steam ships used to anchor. But they anchored outside the reef and used whale or long boats to come all the way down to Nonopapa to land. Nonopapa is a landing, and there were warehouses here. It is further south than Lonopapa.

Leiakauhane. This place is where departed spirits reside. It is a very lovely place and the spirits enjoy many games. If you were hovering between life and death, your *uhane*, or soul, would travel toward this place. Many of the spirits would see you coming and come to greet you. However, if one of your own departed *ohana* saw you, they would escort you back to your body. They would be afraid that if you stayed there, you might not want to leave and thus you would die.

Naalehu (Canoe of Stone). This *moku pohaku* is called Naalehu. It is what the Hawaiians call a *pukoo*, a rock in the ocean, made of *pohaku paakea*, or white sandstone, and this one is said to be a long white canoe.

Na Kanaka Kai (Men from the Sea) or **Na Kanaka Alualu Kai** (Men who Chase the Sea). There seems to be a difference of opinion on what the name of this place should be. A *kupuna*, or elder, by the name of Kaahakila said the name should be Na Kanaka kai. But another *kupuna*, Kalua Keale, said that the name should be Na Kanaka Alualu Kai.

This is Kalua Keale's version of the story about two rocks in the ocean. These two rocks run up out of the water when the water gets rough, and when the water recedes, they run back into the ocean. This is why the name should be Na Kanaka Alualu Kai, the men who chase the sea. This is also a string figure.

Palikahea (The Pali That Calls). This is a cliff where one can call out and get an echo.

Pewahiuiaakekuawalu. Near the cave entrance at the area now called Leahi, one will see embedded on the rock the impression of a fish's tail, possibly a petroglyph. Unfortunately, the story that accompanies this has been forgotten.

Pohakukamaile. This story is about two stones named Kohiapohakuakamaile and Kohiapohakulaau. It is the same as the story of the stones called Koia Uka and Koia Laau, in which they discussed with each other where they wished to remain. One desired to be in the ocean, while the other wanted to be on land. They ended up where they wished to be.

Waiahole (Water of the Ahole). This is an area where the fresh water drips from the rock crevices above down into the ocean below. The *ahole* fish gather around this area, so Niihauans call this fish *aholewai*.

Place Names of Niihau **VII**

The following are Niihau's beach names, starting at Paia and moving clockwise around the island.

Kaluaapuhi	Kaumuhonu	Haleopaweo
Kailioapapai	Kapuaiokana	Lankila
Keanahio	Keanapou	Kiekie
Kahonupilau	Kahalauwaa	Lonopapa
Hatipohue	Kapenakuke	Kalehua
Koiahoolei	Leiakauhane	Halemanuahi
Koiapaakai	Waikai	Keikiakamanawa
Koialaau	Palikahea	Kaununui
Koiauka	Naalehu	Pohakukamaile
Manuauauwai	Kaholonakauupena	Konahina
Malaeahaako	Pewahiuiaakekuawalu	Kaluaakona
Puuohilo	Nakanakaalualukai	Niihauiki
Waiakaulili	Kaluaamalu	Kaaukuu
Waikulu	Kaunuakane	Kalaniwai
Kaholuana	Keanaakoko	Nanina
Waiahole		

The following are Niihau's landings:

Keawalua Landing (near Kamalino)
Keawaiki Landing (at Umeumelua)
Lonopapa Anchorage (at sea for Nonopapa)
Nonopapa Landing (summer landing)
Lehua Landing (at Lehua)
Nanina Landing (at Nanina)
Kaununui Landing (summer landing for supply ships)
Keaukuu (winter landing for supply ships)
Kalaniwai Landing (northern end of island, actually old name of water hole)
Kii Landing (winter landing)
Konahina (flat rock—was considered as a landing at one time)

Kauai to Niihau

Makaweli Landing (at Makaweli, Kauai)
Pupupakai (near Kekaha, Kauai)

Kai ✦ Channels

The following are the channels between Niihau and other islands.

CHANNEL	ISLAND	ISLAND
Kaulakahi	Kauai	Niihau
Kahoomoa	Niihau	Kaula
Kahiowaho	Lehua	Nihoa
Hewa	Kaula	Nihoa

Channel	Island	Island
Manawaanu	Kaula	Lehua
Halii	Lehua	Niihau
Kaieiewaho	Oahu	Kauai
Kaiwi	Oahu	Molokai
Kalohi	Lanai	Kalaau-o-Molokai
Auau	Molokai	Lanai
Pailolo	Maui	Molokai
Kealaikahiki	Lanai	Kahoolawe
Alalakaiki	Maui	Kahoolawe
Alenuihaha	Maui	Hawaii
Hawaii Loa	Nihoa	Necker

Punawai ✦ Springs

The following list of place names identifies *punawai*, or springs and other water sources. Some of the places have been renamed: Keaona is now known as Papataale, Waihuna is now known as Keaona and Waiui is now known as Keapopolo.

Waiakapuaa	Kawaikapu	Makanikahauo
Waiui	Kilomai	Lake Halalii
Haaheo	Kawaieli	Lake Halulu
Waihuna	Waikaheka	Waiakanaio
Waiomina	Kapipi	Waihunaakapaoo (Lehua)
Kaliula	Kapili	Waikulu (Lehua)
Halehaa	Pololonui	Nihoa
Puhala	Manuauauwai	Ekanaulu
Waiaka	Waiakaulili	Ohaiki
Waiakaani	Puuohilo	Waikulu
Hatipohue	Kalehua	Waikai
Pukaitiwaleno	Kalaniwai	

Alii Ponds. Located on the cliffs of Kaali, Alii Ponds is the second largest spring on the island. Taro is grown there today. There is also a pipe carrying water from the spring to Kii.

Hatipohue (*punawai*). This *punawai* or spring is situated on the beach. It once supplied water to the people in the area. To get drinkable water from here, the people would dig a small hole in the sand. As the water filled the hole and overflowed, it would take all the salty water with it and leave drinkable water.

Kalehua. Kalehua is the name of a *punawai* that has lots of good, sweet drinkable water for this area. The water drips into a bowl-shaped rock. The funny thing about this is that the water level always remains the same and the bowl never overflows.

Kaluawaiomakanikoaniani (Makani Kahauo Reservoir). The Robinsons tried unsuccessfully to get government help to drill a well on Niihau, since the island had little water for the cattle. They finally contracted a group of Japanese from Kauai to build this reservoir. They built a stone wall that kept the water in for many years; however, very little of that original wall exists today. Fifteen years ago the whole front of the dam gave way, flooding the entire town of Puuwai.

Keanaulii Stream. Keanaulii, in Puniopo Valley, is Niihau's longest stream at 5.9 miles. Keanaulii is also intermittent.

Lake Halalii. Lake Halalii is an intermittent salt water lake to the east of Lake Halulu. In the rainy season, it swells to as large as 840.7 acres; in the summer, however, it dries up almost entirely.

Lake Halulu. Lake Halulu, the largest natural lake in Hawaii, lies approximately three miles inland from Niihau's southwest shore. A salt water lake, it covers an area of 182 acres. Portions of it dry up during the summer.

Waiakanaio (*punawai*). Waiakanaio is the largest fresh water spring, 500 feet up the north wall of Kanalo Valley. There is a water collection tank at about 570 feet. The ranch pumps water up to about 1,000 feet to supply the cattle.

Waiakanaio Stream. Waiakanaio Stream, in Kanalo Valley, was once the only permanent stream on Niihau. In recent years, it has become intermittent.

Waiakaulili (Water of the Sandpiper). Day after day, the people would watch the *ulili* bird pecking at the reef. Their interest was aroused and they went to see what the bird was doing. They found that he was not pecking at the reef, but was in fact drinking fresh water that was seeping through the reef. Thus they discovered another *punawai* of fresh water.

Waikai (salt water *punawai*). This is a deceptive *punawai*. The water looks like it is good drinking water, but when tasted, it is very salty.

Waikulu (Dripping Waters). *Kulu* means to drip, one drop at a time. At this *punawai*, the water drips into a bowl-shaped rock. The water level always remains the same and the bowl never overflows.

> *Pukaiti wai mapuna aina ike kula manienie* — "Water from Pukaiti lies in a flat meadow."
>
> *Haaheo na wai ekolu Keaona, Waihuna ame Waiui* — "Famous are the three waters Keanona, Waihua and Waiui."

I Noa O Na Wahi Ame Akua
Place Names and the Gods

Hawaiians often named places after legendary heroes, leaders or gods. Over time, the stories behind these names were forgotten. However, the following legendary heroes, demigods or gods are still associated with places on Niihau.

Hiiaka: Paepae o Hiiaka and Poli o Lehua

Hina: Maka o Hina

Kama: Puu o Kama

Kamapuaa and **Pupulenalena**: Kaalipuaa, Waiakapuaa, Kailioopapai, Kamailewalewa, Mauuloa, Mahuuaawi, Waiu, Kaholeinapuaa and Kawaiakailio

Kana: Ka puai o Kana

Kane: Ka unu a Kane

Kapo: Kapo hoa lii lii; Kapo hakau, Puni a Kapo (valley), Kapo hakau (ledge) and Kapo laau

Ku: Ke ana o Ku; Lae o Ku (near Kahalekua) and Maka o Ku (*heiau*, Nuololo, Kauai)

Liloa: Paepae kapu o Liloa

Lono: Lono i Kahiki

Maui: Ka lua o Maui

Pele: Kaluaakawila (Pele's first pit digging) and Motupapa

CHAPTER VIII

Place Names of *Lehua, Kaula & Nihoa*

*He aloha Nihoa i ka ehu kai
aka Naulu ae hiipoi nei*

Beloved is Nihoa in the salt spray
Courted by the Naulu winds

Cave shelters on island of Nihoa. (*Photo: Bishop Museum*)

Place Names of Lehua, Kaula and Nihoa VIII

*A*BOUT ONE-HALF MILE north of Niihau is the rocky, crescent-shaped islet of Lehua. The eastern and western coasts are low, gradually rising to 702 feet in elevation. The southern side has gullies, wave cliffs and a cave. Southern access is also restricted by numerous rocks above sea level that extend almost halfway across the channel Halii to Niihau. Near the western point is Keaulepe, a natural arch. Kaunuokala is the highest point on Lehua, and the highest lighthouse in the U.S. Lighthouse Service exists here. At one time, the island was overrun with rabbits and a few still remain. Some of the birds on the island include *noio, uau kane* and *akekeke*.

On Lehua there are two *punawai:* Waihunaakapaoo and Halii. There are also two landings. The Moae is the wind of the island. Many people once lived on Lehua. After the people of Niihau heard that their island was up for sale to the *haole,* many left for Lehua. From there, they carried on their trade with other islands via the boat *Kaiaoni.* There are fifteen place names for Lehua:

Kaunuakala	Naupaka
Halii (*punawai* and landing)	Papaloa
Waihunaakapaoo (*punawai*)	Waikulu
Kanukuapuaa	Keanamoi
Kahauna	Keananoio
Keaulepe	Kapoliolehua
Minolii	Kukaiaiki
Kalokoakaha	

Anakukaiaiki. The cave home of the shark *aumakua* Kukaiaiki. It is said about the channel between Kauai and Niihau that "if you fall into the Kaulakahi Channel close to Niihau, you will be safe. If you fall into the channel near Kauai, God will help you." Kuhaiaiki protected the people of Niihau. Long ago, a pact was made with this shark *aumakua,* and the people should never fear for their lives as long as they were in this realm.

Ka leina aka uhane o ko Niihau poe uhane (The Leaping Place for Souls of the People of Niihau). According to legend, Mauloku was the *milu* or jumping off place for souls. It is not remembered just where this is.

Kanukuapuaa. This point has the appearance of a pig's snout.

Kaunuakala. The highest point on Lehua.

Keanamoi. This cave is where the *moi* fish gather.

Keananoio. The cave of the *noio* bird.

Keaulepe. It is said that a man tried to pry the land apart to prove his love, but it took him two attempts.

Halii. Once a boat landing area. Also name of a fine *punawai* and channel between Lehua and Niihau.

Waihunaakapaoo (*punawai*). In the old days, fresh water would drip off the rocks very slowly and run out to the ocean. The people did not know that this was fresh water. The fish would climb up into the cracks and hide themselves, and when the men visited the area, the fish scampered off, jumping back into the ocean. The strange behavior of these little fish was noticed and when the men went to investigate, they found the fresh water. So they cleaned out the crevices in the rock and built a little *punawai* to catch the water for drinking. With water so precious and sparse, all *punawai* were kept clean and cared for. The reason for the name is because the little fish kept these waters for themselves and hid it—thus the name, the Hidden Waters of the Paoo. *Paoo* is believed to be the fish now known as *panoo*, very similar to *oopu kai* in the tide pools. This *punawai* is still in existence. However, since no one depends on this water for survival, people have stopped caring for it and the birds have taken over.

Papaloa. "Long Reef"

Waikulu. "Dripping Waters." Fresh water seeps from these rocks.

> *Kapoliolehua* — "Cradled in the bosom of Lehua." Used when speaking of the Pele family; Hiiaka is said to have left a *lehua* flower there on her first visit.
>
> *Aia i ka mole o lehua* — "At the foundation of Lehua." Said of one who has been gone a long time; the foundation is Niihau. From *Olelo Noeau*, by Mary Pukui.
>
> *Ke hao aela ka makani koa pua ia o Lehua* — "The wind beats Lehua, barrenness is her flower."

Kaula

The island of Kaula is approximately nineteen miles southwest of Niihau, across the Kahoomoa Channel. It is a small, rocky islet with its highest point 550 feet above sea level. It contains between 108 and 136 acres. The U.S. Lighthouse Service formerly maintained an automatic beacon on the islet. This beacon was the second highest in the U.S. Lighthouse Service—it stood 562 feet above sea level. There are many birds, mainly terns and boobys, on this islet; many migrate from Niihau. There are more than fifteen different species of plants. This islet was a special rendezvous for the people during the summer months when they went to catch birds or to fetch olivine for their octopus lures. The natives of Niihau thought more of visiting Kaula than they thought of visiting Oahu or Kauai. In ancient times, Kaula was inhabited.

The Niihau association with Kaula has been a long one. The name often appears in old *mele* and legends. It has always been regarded as a very special place. It was one of the favorite places of Kane. In the language of the priesthood, reference to the west Kalakau really meant Kaula. Kaulanaula, as Kaula was known by early Niihauans, refers to the arc belonging to the red, or *alii*. Kaula, Nihoa and Niihau are the three islands claimed by the red line or royal *alii* of the *ahuula*, the highest *alii* blood lines.

It was very common in ancient days to have observation posts in order to spot any advancing enemies. Niihau was the center point. The chief's vantage point on Niihau was on Puu Kaeo. From here one could look down towards Kaununui and directly toward Nihoa. The plateau known as Kiekie on Niihau was the lookout from where they could observe Kaula. As the men from Niihau approached Kaula, they would observe the actions of the birds. If the birds were acting erratic, they knew trouble was on the way.

The men of Niihau would, as custom dictates, pay their respects to the great shark god from Tahiti, Kuhaimoana. There was a ritual done by the paddlers. They would scale the cliffs and head for the *heiau* Kahalauloa, Kaunu and Pohakupio, which are directly above the cave Keanaoku. This cave is approximately 200 feet deep.

The people had a very unique way of climbing up the sheer cliffs. The *opihi* were plentiful and very large, so they would only have to tap the *opihi*, which causes the shellfish to cling to the rock, thus creating a natural ladder to climb, hence the name Kealaakaopihi. Ekeeke is the west wind of Kaula.

While the lighthouse was being built, the men found the cliffs difficult to climb so one man erected a ladder. After reaching the top of the islet, some thirty feet above the ocean, he was washed off the cliff by a large wave. He was washed off the island, said an old Niihau man, because it is customary to first pay your respects at the cave, Keanaoku, before going onto the islet, and this man did not!

> *Ailana o Kaula i ka mole olu home pohai mau ana manu* — "The island of Kaula is the ancestral home of the birds."
>
> *Eia Kaula leo la, he waimaka, aloha mai o Kaulanaulu* — "Here is the voice and tears of Kaula, welcome to Kaulanaula (the red *alii* line)."
>
> *Aina o Kaula i ke komohana hoa paio no ke Konahea* — "To the west, Kaula the island and opponent of the Konahea wind."

The place names of Kaula—*Na inoa malua o Kaula Waho*—are:

Kahuku	Koekeeke	Keahu
Maio	Kealaakaopihi	Kahoomoa
Pohakupio (*heiau*)	Keananoio	Nehoa
Kaunu (*heiau*)	Kumukoa	Keawaiki
Papala	Manohua	Kaneneenee
Pali-a-Kane	Waiula	Kahalauloa (*heiau*)
Keanaoku		

Nihoa

Although Nihoa is about 120 miles northwest of Niihau, it plays a very important part in Niihau's history. Nihoa has a land area of 156 acres. Its highest point is 910 feet in elevation. Along the north, east and west shores are sheer cliffs up to 850 feet high. The people of Niihau explained that their forefathers traveled frequently to Nihoa, as this was one of the stopovers during trips to and from Tahiti. Tutu Kaui said that the route traveled was from Niihau to Nihoa to Motu Papapa and then Tahiti. Asked where Motu Papapa was, Tutu Kaui and Tia Kapahu said, "It is about halfway to Tahiti."

Though the island is barren and rocky, archaeological sites on Nihoa substantiate that ancient peoples lived there, as Dr. Kenneth Emory of the Bishop Museum found. He noted in "Humans on Nihoa 553 Years Ago" (*Honolulu Advertiser*, 1956) that there were remains of houses and evidence of food crops. The population of Nihoa in 1779 was approximately 4,000 *kanaka*.

The Niihauans were frequent visitors and knew the best landing. If on a particular day they wished to go fishing on Nihoa, they would climb up Puu Kaeo on Niihau where there is a marker and look out towards Nihoa. If weather conditions permitted the trip, they would leave by canoe from Kaununui, taking with them provisions and gourds of fresh water. When they reached Nihoa, they had good, sweet water from a large *punawai* called Waiakanohoaka. They landed on a beach on the south side of the island. Other trips to Nihoa were to collect leaves and wood for spears from the *loulu* palm that grew only on Nihoa, and to bring back a fiber-like grass, *makiukiu*, that was used for cord and stuffing.

The island was also used as a place for young lovers—a chance to be alone and get to know one another. The last couple to visit was named Kaaumoana. The Niihauans sailed to Nihoa in the spring winds, returning to Niihau in the fall on Kona winds.

In 1822, Kaahumanu and her royal party—Liholiho, Kaumualii, Keopuokalani and Kahekili Keeaumoku—left Kauai for Niihau where they were royally entertained. Kaahumanu had only heard of Nihoa in *mele* and legends, since the island was unknown to her generation. The people of Niihau at that time told stories and legends of Nihoa and its importance to them. So Kaahumanu asked that they join her party in proving that the island existed and that it had been occupied prior to the eighteenth century, even though by the end of the eighteenth century it was all but forgotten. When Kaahumanu and her royal party visited Nihoa, Captain William Sumner took possession of the island for her.

In remembrance of the visit that Kaahumanu made to Nihoa with Kaumualii, she named the waterfront between Kaahumanu Street and her Nuuanu home on Oahu after Nihoa. Later, Princess Liliuokalani made a visit to Nihoa. She was quite astonished to find remnants of a village, sweet potatoes, yams and other plants. She also noted the *heiau*.

> *Ku paku ka pali o Nihoa i kamakani* — "The cliffs of Nihoa stand as a resistance against the wind." Said of a person who stands bravely in the face of misfortune.
>
> *He aloha Nihoa i ka ehu kai Aka Naulu ae hiipoi nei* — "Beloved is Nihoa in the salt spray courted by the Naulu winds."
>
> *He puu kolo i Nihoa* — "Climbing the cliffs of Nihoa." Men who visited there had to find ways to crawl up the cliffs.

These are some names of the islands beyond Nihoa, but it is not remembered which island was which:

Mokuakamohoalii
Hanakaieie
Hanakeaumoe
Ununui

Afterword

The music of Niihau has a special spiritual quality that evokes a stirring sense of "being Hawaiian." Indeed, the Niihau a cappella choral singing is reminiscent of the true South Pacific. For the most part, the voices are untrained and people sing with unrestrained voices—singing in the way of the *kanaka kahiko*, or people of old, sometimes using only two or three tones in the entire song. At times, the rhythm appears to differ throughout the song.

Music is essential to Niihau. Almost everyone plays the *ukulele* or guitar and there are even three distinct Niihau styles of slack-key music. One particular style of slack-key is derived from an old style of playing brought from Kohala, Hawaii. Their songs also reflect older melodies that in many cases have been forgotten, though some tunes have become popular on other islands. These songs include "Waiakanaio," "Ua Mau," "Pupu o Niihau," "Nani Niihau," "Kawaihoa," "Kahelelani," "Poe Koa o Niihau," "Lauapine," "Kanaka Waiwai," "Aloha ka Manini," "Papa Sia" and "Kaulana Niihau."

Life is changing on Niihau. Time transforms even this remote "forbidden island." The *kupuna* whose legends, stories, histories and lore have been preserved here are the last remaining bridge to the living memory of old Hawaii. Their words are music that sing to us of faith, values and respect for the sacred land, ocean and sky. As Hawaii's people face the challenges of the twenty-first century, the haunting music of this island community will hopefully be a source of enjoyment, knowledge and love.

School children at Puuwai, 1925. (*Photo: Bishop Museum*)

Appendix A

List of Residents of Nihoa on March 7, 1884

In a letter to C.J. Judd, Minister of the Interior, an M. Kukuanoa listed all the residents living on Nihoa then. They have been there long before the days of Kaahumanu until Kinau. Some of these persons were originally from Niihau.

Kaluahinenui	Kana	Kumukala	Kuke
Paka	Laki	Kahewahewanui	Kaluaamohi
Kaiana	Keoni	Nahehaku	Kumupala
Kukae	Kahaloa	Kaluahumenui	Nakahalau
Naiwi	Leleaka	Pihiliilii	Kailiino
Namai	Haole	Palaiu	Kauana

Source: *Hawaii State Archives*

APPENDIX B

Letters to the Minister of the Interior, 1863 & 1864

Niihau was originally monarchy land except for some small parcels. For many years the Niihauans tried to purchase or lease the island's land. Some received lands in the Great Mahele of 1848 and many others had leases with the Hawaiian government. A new government agent arrived and raised the land lease rates to unheard-of prices, making it necessary for some to move off the island in yet another migration to Kauai, in 1858. They had a friend on Kauai who tried to help by sending letters to the Minister of Interior. There are also many letters from Puko, Kauukualii and Wahineaea in the Hawaii State Archives that speak of leasing or outright purchase. In the later part of 1863, when the people heard the island was to be sold to *haole malihini*, they again argued in letters that the island land be sold to them instead. These letters follow. In 1864, still more people moved away to Hawaii, Maui, and Kauai.

Letter One

To the Minister of the Interior, G.M. Robertson, from S. Nawaalaau, spokesman for the people of Niihau, January 1864.

We the makaainanas of your island of Niihau write this letter to ask you to stand behind us as we hear rumors that Niihau will be sold to the haole. Please help us to purchase the land, please do not go and stand with the malihinis. We are all concerned that if the island is sold to the malihinis our way of living will not be the same and possibly be very foreign to us. If you have any doubts about this request, we would be happy to send you a list of all the kamaainas that support this paper.

Letter Two

To the Minister of the Interior, G.M. Robertson, from the eight leaders of the community, September 22, 1863.

We request an appointment with the Minister to discuss the rental or purchase of Niihau, because a lot of the kamaainas are leaving and moving off the island due to the haoles. P.R. Holi is elected to represent the people ... The kamaainas that are left are ill, old and weak. The total real residents on Niihau now are 111.

APPENDIX

Niihau Family Names During the 1800s

This list of names accompanied Letter Two.

Adamu	Kalalau	Kenika
Amosa	Kalana	Koakanu
Anadarea	Kalo	Kohu
Anekalea	Kalua	Kou
Asa	Kamapua	Kounui
Ehu	Kamawaho	Ku
Haiakua	Kanahele	Kuahine
Haiole	Kanakuiki	Kuamio
Hakaimee	Kaneapua	Kuhalau
Hakamee	Kaneiki	Kukahaka
Halalau	Kanewahine	Kukahika
Hanuhanu	Kaohelaulii	Kukuele
Harada	Kaomea	Kula
Heleinamoku	Kaona	Kula
Hina	Kaopulua	Lawai
Hokea	Kapahee	Lihau
Holi	Kapahiiki	Luaehu
Holo	Kapahu	Luiomana
Hopea	Kapahulehua	Mahele
Huamio	Kapio	Mahina
Hulu	Kapuaiki	Mahiole
Huluhulu	Kapule	Makaualani
Iara	Kapuulau	Makaulani
Kaaukulipuhi	Karoiki	Mamuli
Kaaukuu	Kauaiki	Mana
Kaeo	Kauanaulu	Maunui
Kahala	Kauhi	Metekio
Kahale	Kauiki	Metekio(a)
Kahalemaile	Kaukini	Mikioi
Kahele	Kaulei	Nakao
Kahokuloa	Kauohai	Namaka
Kaholemaile	Kauolua	Namakualike
Kaholomaile	Kawahine	Nameania
Kahopealoha	Kawaiula	Naneakea
Kaiaua	Kawika	Naona(Kaona)
Kaiko	Keahi	Nawaalaau
Kaikuahine	Kealaula	Niheu
Kaikuakini	Keale	Niihau
Kaulau	Keamoai	Nohokula
Kailianu	Keanakaikii	Nuuhiva
Kaina	Keauaiki	Nuuhiwa

Ohao	Pookina	Puni
Pahuole	Puai	Shintani
Pakapa	Puhiula	Toma
Palupaakai	Pukaa	Wahineaea
Papapa	Pukau	Waiaki
Pauiki	Puke	Wehea
Petero	Puko	Wehekeala
Peteroiki	Pula	Zakaio
Poohiwa	Punene	Zakania

Appendix C

Royal Patent No. 2944

Kamehameha V to James McHutcheson Sinclair and Frances Sinclair
Ten Thousand Dollars

The whole of the lands now belonging to the Government on the island of Niihau. It being understood that under this patent the whole of the land on the said island of Niihau is conveyed to the said James McHutchenson Sinclair and Francis Sinclair with the exception of the two lands known as Kahuku and Halawela, set off the Koakanu in the great Division of 1848, and that tract of land sold to Papapa, containing fifty acres, which is more pertinently described in Royal Patent # 1615 of Land Sales. That patent, in the diagram also describes the pieces of land set apart for Church and school lots, and also excepting and reserving to the Hawaiian Government, all mineral and Metallic mines of every description.

To have and to hold the above granted land in Fee Simple unto said James McHutchenson Sinclair and Francis Sinclair, their heirs and assigns forever as Tenants in Common. Subject to the Taxes to be from time to time imposed by the Legislative Councils, equally upon all landed property held in fee simple.

In witness wherefore, I have hereunto set my hand and caused the great seal of the Hawaiian Islands to be affixed at Honolulu this 23rd day of February A.D. 1864.

KAMEHAMEHA R. by the King and Kuhina Nui

G.M. Robertson
M. Kekuanaoa

Source: *Hawaii Dept. of Land and Natural Resources*

APPENDIX D
Moena Pawehe Designs

PAHAKU

KUHANU

LEI HALA

NENE

PAPAULA

OLOWAHIA

HUMU UMITI

PUAKALA

NIHO WILI HEMO

KIKEE

HIU

APPENDIX 113

HONU

NIHO MANO

PEPEHI HALUA

IWI PUHI

PAPA KONANE

HALE

NANA NUU

114   NIIHAU: The Traditions of a Hawaiian Island

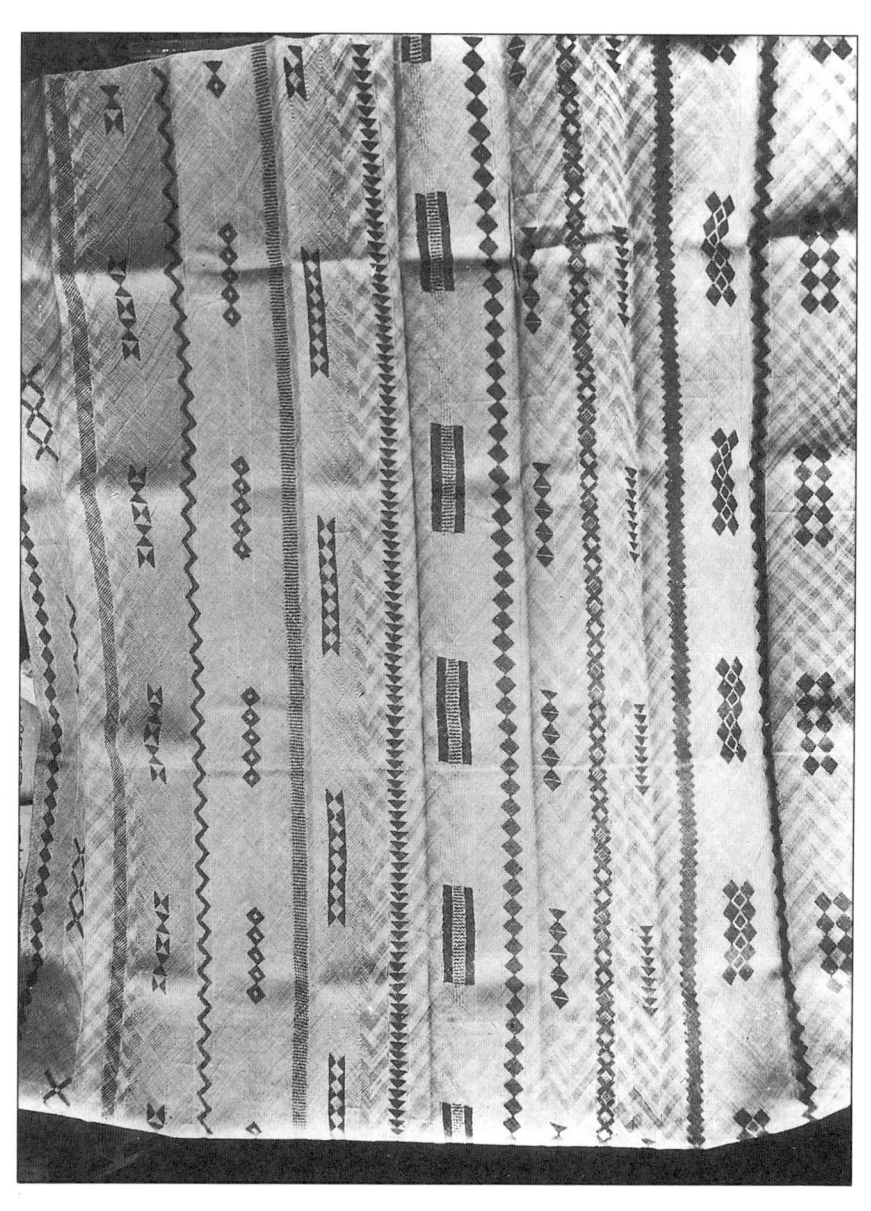

Moena Pawehe — makaloa mat (*Photo: Bishop Museum*)

Glossary

Words or pronunciations unique to Niihau are in capital letters

aa, rough lava
aho, heavy cord
ahole, fish
ahupuaa, land division
ahuula, royal feather cloak
aina, land
ake, liver
akekeke, bird
akeloa, spleen
aku, skipjack
akua, god
alaea, red clay
ALIA, type of spear
alii, royal persons
aloha, greeting, love
ama, canoe outrigger
ame, and
ana, cave
anaana, sorcery
aumakua, family guardian
auwe, exclamation, *Alas!*
awa, ceremonial drink
awaawa, valley

buke, book

ehu, reddish, ruddy complexion
eiwa, nine
elima, five

hake okeo, jump rope
haku, composed, made by
hala, pandanus, gone

hale, house
halakahiti, pineapple
halalu, small fish
halau, long house
hale pule, church
halepili, thatched house
haole, foreigner
HAUNA, chum for fishing
HAVANA, palm seeds
hee, octopus
hee nalu, surfing
hei, string figure, game
hele, come, go
helua, self defense
heiau, ancient temple
himeni, song, hymn
hinahina, silversword
hipa, sheep
hiuia, fish tail
holoholona, animals
honu, turtle
hoolehua, act of sliding, sled
hoomana, religion
hua, fruit
huewai, water gourd
hula, dance
humuhumunukunukuapuaa, small fish
huna, hidden

ihe, spear
ilalo, downward, down
ili, land section

ilima, native shrub
ilio, dog
ilioholoikauaua, seal
iluna, up, upward
ina, sea urchins
imu, earth oven
ipu, gourd
iwi, bone

kaa, small cord
kaao, legendary stories
kahito, old, ancient
kahu, keeper, pastor
kahuna, learned one, sorcerer
kai, sea, sea water, channel
kalae, point
Kalavina, Calvinistic
kalua, roast in earth oven
kamaaina, native born
kamakani, winds
kanaka, man, human being
kane, man
Kane, a god
kaona, hidden meaning
kapa kuiki, Hawaiian quilt
kapu, forbidden
kapuai, footprint
kapulu, unclean
kaua, weapon, war
kaukaualii, class of chiefs
kaunaoa, morning glory
kauwa, slave
keiti, keiki, child, champion
kiawe, Algeroba tree
kii, petroglyphs
kilo, reader of omens, seer
kilu, game
kinikini, marbles
kipona, multi-color lei
ko, sugar cane

kohekohe, a reed
koko, blood, net
kona, leeward
KUIKUI, candlenut tree (kukui)
kula, dry land
kulu, to drip (as water)
kumu, teacher
ku polou, pole vaulting
kupua, supernatural beings
kupuna, ancestors, elders

la, sun, there
laau, medicine tree
lauae, fragrant fern
lauhala, leaf of pandanus tree
lawaia, fishing
Lehua, island
lehua, flower
lei, shell or flower garland
lepo, dirt
limu, seaweed
loa, long
loina, rules
loko, pond
LONO MATAIHE, spear throwing
loulu, palm
lua, pit, hole
Lua, art of self defense
lua kupapau, burial caves
luau, feast
luna, headman, boss, foreman

mahalo, to thank, thanks
mahiai, to farm
mahu, hermaphrodite
maile, fragrant twining shrub
makaloa, a sedge
makani, wind
makau, fishhook

Glossary

makaula, prophet
MAKIUKIU, grass from Nihoa
malihini, newcomer
malina, sisal plant
malo, loin cloth
MALUA, pit, hole
mawaena, between
mana, spirit, power
mano, shark
manu, bird
mauka, towards the mountain
mea, thing, article
mele, chant, song
METI, iron
Milu, underworld
moi, fish
momi, shell, pearl
moo, lizard
MOE, sleep
moena, mat
moku, island, ship
mole, base of, root, foundation
moo, lizard
motu, island
Mu, ancient public executioners, silent ones
muumuu, long dress

na mea hana, tools
na mea hana lima, arts and crafts
na mea kaua, weapons
na mea paani, sports
NEKI, great bulrush, reed
nenue, a fish
Nihoa, island
noio, Hawaiian tern
nui, large

o, of
ohana, family

ohe kahiki, Tahitian bamboo
ohia, type of wood
olaa, to wilt over fire
olelo, speech, word, language
olelo nane, riddle
olelo noeau, poetic saying
olona, native shrub
oopu, goby fish
opae, shrimp
opihi, shellfish, limpet
opu, stomach

pa, fence
paakai, salt
pai, ancient game
pakea, plain mat
palaoa, necklace
paepae, platform
pahoehoe, smooth lava
pali, cliff
panapua, arrow
papa, reef, foundation
PAPAIPAAKEA, type of crab
PAPIPI, cactus
PAUA, pearl shell
pau, empty, finish
PAWEHE, design
pikake, peacock, jasmine flower
pikoilua, dagger
pili, type of grass
pilo, Hawaiian spider lily
poe, people
poepoe, lei rope style
pohaku, stone
pohue, gourd
poi, tuber starch staple
POKEOKEO, turkey
POOWAWAE, turned head to foot
pua, baby mullet, flower
puaa, pig

118 *NIIHAU: The Traditions of a Hawaiian Island*

pueo, owl
puhala, pandanus tree
puhi, eel
puka, gate, opening
pukoo, rock in ocean
pule, prayer
pule kala, forgiveness
punawai, water spring
pupu, shell
puu, hill, mound
puuhonua, place of refuge
puuwai, heart
Puuwai, name of town

tapa, bark cloth
taro, tuber, food staple
tautau, tattoo
TII, image
tiki, image
TOHETOHE, a reed
TOHOLA, whale

TUMU, tree
TUPUNA, elders, ancestors
Tutu, grandparent

uaukane, bird
uhane, soul
uhi, yam
ukulele, musical instrument
ula, red
ulu, breadfruit
uluna, pillow
UMETE, calabash, bowl
umu, earth oven
unu, altar
uwala, sweet potato

waa, canoe
wai, water
wahine, woman
wili, twisted
wiliwili, tree

BIBLIOGRAPHY

Barrere, Dorothy B., Mary Kawena Pukui and Marion Kelly. *Hula: Historical Perspectives.* Honolulu: Bishop Museum Record #30, 1980.

Beaglehole, J.C. *The Life of Captain James Cook.* Stanford, Calif: Stanford University Press, 1974.

Beckwith, Martha. *Hawaiian Mythology.* Honolulu: University of Hawaii Press, 1970.

Bishop Museum Occasional Papers, XVII, 1913.

Brigham, William T. "Mat and Basket Weaving of Ancient Hawaiians". Honolulu: Bishop Museum Bulletin #11, 1906.

Bolton, H. "Some Hawaiian Pastimes". 1892.

Bryan, E.H.J. *Ancient Hawaiian Life.* 1903.

Dickey, Lyle A. "String Figures of Hawaii". Bishop Museum Bulletin #54, 1928.

Dodge, Ernest S. *Hawaiian and Other Polynesian Gourds.* Honolulu: Topgallant, 1978.

Ellis, William. *Journal of William Ellis, Narrative of a Tour of Hawaii.* Rutland, Vermont: Charles Tuttle Press, 1979.

Emerson, Nathaniel B. *Unwritten Literature of Hawaii: The Sacred Songs of the Hula.* Rutland, Vermont: Charles Tuttle Press, 1965.

Emory, Kenneth P. "Archaeology of Nihoa and Necker". Honolulu: Bishop Museum Bulletin #53.

Forbes, Charles. Bishop Museum Occasional Papers, Vol. 3, 1913.

Fornander, Abraham. *Fornander Collection of Hawaiian Antiquities and Folk-Lore.* Honolulu: Bishop Museum Press, 1916-1920.

Handy, E.S. Craighill and Elizabeth G. Handy. "Native Planters in Old Hawaii; Their Life, Lore, and Environment". Honolulu: Bishop Museum Press, 1972.

Hawaii State Data Book, The. 1981.

Hawaiian Mission Children's Society Library: Church Reports, 1867.

Teriura, Henry. "Ancient Tahiti". Honolulu: Bishop Museum Bulletin #48.

Hillebrand, William. *Flora of the Hawaiian Islands.* London: Norgate, 1888.

Hinds, Norman H. "Geology of Kauai and Ni'ihau". Honolulu: Bishop Museum Bulletin #71.

Hiroa, Te Rangi. "Arts and Crafts". Honolulu: Bishop Museum Bulletin #45.

Honolulu Advertiser (Pacific Commercial Advertiser): 1934, 1900, 1890, 1864.

King, James. *Captain James Cook*. London: W.&A. Streahan, 1784.

Niihau Ledgers, in Hawaiian.

Official Census Reports from the Kingdom of Hawaii.

Palmer, Harold S. *Geology of Kaula and Lehua*. Honolulu: Bishop Museum.

Pukui, Mary Kawena. "Ancient Hula of Kaua`i." *Garden Isle* newspaper, 1936.

Pukui, Mary Kawena. *Olelo Noeau*. Honolulu: Bishop Museum Press, 1983.

Republic of Hawaii, U.S. Bureau of Census and the Sandwich Islands Mission Reports.

Rodman, Julius. *Kahuna Sorcerers*. Hicksville, New York: Exposition Press, 1979.

Sinclair, Francis, Jr. *Indigneous Flowers of Hawaii*. London: Leighton Brothers, 1885.

Map Index

There are more than 938 place names on the small island of Niihau. With time and events, some old names were replaced with new ones. This is the most complete record of the older names of Niihau that were recorded in the ledgers. They have never before been published and thus preserved. Only a few have been mapped prior to this effort. These names often have several meanings: literal, physical quality, and legendary association.

Because a map that would indicate all of Niihau's place names would be too large to include in this book, we have developed a method of indexing place names. In this index, place names are divided into sections corresponding to numbers and letters on the map. In each section, names are listed in geographic order. Numbered sections refer to places on or near Niihau's coast, while sections with letters refer to inland locations. Certain key locations are noted directly on the map for reference. In this way, we hope to preserve the place names of Niihau and their locations.

The numbered sections below are close to the beach, starting at Paia and continuing southward. ***The map is on pages 130 and 131.***

SECTION 1
Paia
Hanai
Kaluapuhi
Owai
Kailioopapai
Iheihekahi
Kuinakaiole
Kapaoaohalalii
Pakahi
Palua
Keawaau
Uwela
Kiao
Akaka
Kahekawaiauau
Kawa
Kepuhi (1)
Pipipiakolea
Pipipieleele

Keawakalai
Pooneone

SECTION 2
Kalolo
KaluaPahapaha
Kahonu
Kapapaokukui
Kawaaloa
Papaloa
Kaulana (kalae)
Apu
Oiamoi

SECTION 3
Kapae
Kahauka
Kilia
Kalaau
Mahu
Paena

Kiolapaakea
Keanahio
Kahonupilau
Mahunaiwi (1)
Mahunaiwi (2)
Kapohaku
Kalanei
Alakauwa
Keananoio
Keaku
Kalepe
Namahana
Pahala
Keanamoi
Peeloa
Makaohina
Kuloloa
Lehei
Kepuhi (2)
Koahe (kalae)

NOTE: *Several places have the same names, i.e. a name is often used for more than one location. Names that are followed by a number refer to places of similar names either in the same or in another section or area.*

SECTION 4
Kaluamalu
Hatipohue (punawai)
Amakakeiki (1)
Laeokona
Laeokaia
Kahiohio
Kahooleinakanaka
Kanakamoli
Koiahoolei
Koiapaakai
Koialaau
Koiauka
Amakakeiki (2)
Leholiilii
Pohakuokamaile
Kealea

SECTION 5
Keanahaki
Keawaiki
Keawanui
Manuauauwai (punawai)
Malaeahaaka (punawai)
Puuohilo (punawai)
Waiakaulili (punawai)
Waikulu (1) (punawai)
Paepae o Hiiaka
Poliolehua
Poliahu
Kahauka (kalae)
Poikaohu
Aikeana
Kaohinailiili
Kaholopuaiwa
Kiihelei
Kapae
Kaaulana (kalae)
Kaunuakala (Kawaihoa)
Kawaihoa

SECTION 6
Papanui
Papapioanenue

Kaholuana
Pukaamoe
Waikapoli
Waikulu (2)
Waiahole
Kaumuhonu

SECTION 7
Kapuai o Kana
Keoneanapa
Keanapou
Kahalauwaa
Kapena Kuke
Kuhumu
Kahauka
Waikulu (3)
Kealahula
Leinakauhane
Leiwalo
Kamauu
Pohakuokamaile
Kaopaka
Kealea
Waikai
Kahauna
Kepuhi (3)
Kanalohuluhulu
Kaoweakawai
Kahanuakauwila
Kaanawaa
Pulekoa
Palikahea
Kealea
Keahi
Kelelo
Kaloaloa
Naalehu (moku pohaku)
Poo
Kaholonakaupena
Keaki
Keanapuka
Halo
Kalaekahi
Keahu

Kiieenana
Kalanei
Keanaakamanu
Kuinaakaopihi
Kahai
Kulepe
Kuakelii
Pewahiuiaakekuawalu
Paialanai
Kaumekeaiahina
Kawaaloa
Nakanakakai
Leahi

SECTION 8
Kalunakoa
Keaku
Kaluamalu
Nukupee
Kaluapuhi
Kaluapahee
Papaloa
Makapohaku
Akahiakahi
Haikaena
Kaluawai
Papalekohe
Kalepeamoa
Kaumakani (1)
Kaelinawi

SECTION 9
Kaluaahole
Kulanakoeho
Kalaeokaia
Namahana (2)
Kaumakani (2)
Kaakaluamalu
Kukapoli
Pohakunui
Polimalo
Kahaino

SECTION 10
Kaliilii

MAP INDEX 123

Ioioa
Keahu
Waikiu
Kuhilua
Kelo
Kealoonakii
Opuonakii
Kipapa
Namaha (3)
Kapukaone
Hokukauwelowelo
Okolehoolea
Lanaikahiki (pohaku)
Luahiwa
Inanui
Pahaunui
Pahauiki
Kaholaiki
Huawaiakanukupo-
 loulo
Puhiula (pohaku)
Kuaakapu
Kuaaapa
Kuawaalua
Kahili
Umeumelua
Kaanakau
Haenui
Laulau
Kamahina
Kaluakomo
Keawaula
Kawaiki
Kekawanui
Kaunu a Kaane
Kaluamalu (2)
Keakole
Keanakoko
Haleopaweo (Keale)
Papaiki
Keanaakauwila
Kuamanu
Kioopa

Makaopihi
Lanakila (hale pule)
Keawaiki
Kiloia
Kamalino

SECTION 11

Kaukauaiwa
Kahuakawi
Nehoa
Laeoku
Kahalekua
Namahana (3)
Maloe
Kawa
Kawi
Lele
Kealea
Pia
Kahololua
Kiekiei
Kaholua
Kamaluhi
Namanamana
Waahia
Kukahi
Kahoomoa
Kamauu
Kaumakani
Nahalekahi
Kahalauloa
Keoneopololi
Kanaele
Kapika
Lonoikahiki
Anuenue
Kealohipapa
Hale o Lonopapa
Kuamanamana
Kahekapalahalaha
Ohikaalu
Kiao
Pohakuloa
Manawaiki

Kaohinailiili
Kahuawaihi
Keakole
Kanaha
Kina
Papaiki
Halo
Papaloa
Pakaua

SECTION 12

Kawa (ihupa)
Keawakau
Uwalakahiki
Halawela
Kuloa
Kuinaipu
Kuaakamoku

SECTION 13

Keahi
Alalipoa
Kapae
Halehaa
Kaiwimoeonakupuna
Kauhiwaa
Kaluakanaka
Hualele
Apopo
Opelau
Halepuleopalani
Kalua o Maui
Moihewa
Paliuli (kalae)

SECTION 14

Keana o Ku
Kuaapa
Keawaaulukou
Kaumemai
Kapaiwi
Papaiki
Papakahi
Pueo
Lilaakalei

Nenuelele
Pao
Kainuminumi
Puheheke
Hoolelekawa
Kaalea
Kamoilehua
Kaluahonu
Kamoamoa

SECTION 15
Apu
Lua
Paki
Kolonaiwi
Napaka (i hupe)
Kauhipohaku
Kuawaalua
Papakahi (2)
Papamuku
Puaikeakua
Kawahamano
Moemoe
Ohianalukaulana
Kepa
Hapalua
Anaanakau
Kapiko
Pikonui
Kahio
Pikouha
Keawakauaohao
Kalehu
Kaaieahulikoola
Kawahamano
Kapukaakoolau
Kalanei

SECTION 16
Kapiko (2)
Akiakipo
Kalauliilii
Puu o Kama
Kaumakani

Kaholeinapuaa
Kalehua
Kepuhi
Keanapuka
Kalualena
Namanamana
Nakeikiaeiakamanawa
Waiapalo
Keawaakakanehaole
Kauwaha
Kaununui

SECTION 17
Kaa
Kepuhi (2)
Nenuelele
Puhioloolo
Wanawana
Kaluamalu
Keanapuka
Waiakailio
Halalii
Namahana
Kukaelama
Kuikui
Pohakuakamaile
Kawelo
Kuhohai
Haenaloa
Pakala
Konahina
Kaluakomo
Keawanui
Kealaae
Kahekawaiauau
Malakeiki
Halulu

SECTION 18
Puukoae
Kuhialii
Kaunuakapua
Kihawahine

SECTION 19
Hakea
Ahualoa
Kewaakule
Kupeahi
Niihauiki
Kawaiaina
Nawaalua
Kawahaehu
Kaaukuu
Mokuaweoweo
Keawaakaniela
Kaunuohiki
Kaunuokaha
Kealohi
Kalaniwai
Kalanihale
Puukole (kahai)
Keapaheehee
Kahalekuamano
Kapapawai
Makalepo

SECTION 20
Nanina
Keamano
Pahele
Keawaula
Kikepa

SECTION 21
Paheleuka
Kalaelipaakai
Nohonoa
Kapoahole
Kapohoaleilei
Kapolaau
Inanui
Papakoahe
Kapunawai
Keahu
Kahololoa
Kepuhi (3)
Kaunupou

MAP INDEX

Kahoololo

SECTION 22
Papakiekie
Home o Kii
Kaluamalu
Kapalawai
Kalehu
Moikoiu
Kanahawele
Kamoa
Apu
Keawakee
Hoolualoa
Nopai
Poleho

SECTION 23
Kealakekao
Kekelahewaa
Kalaeloa
Halona
Mahulu
Kiikapae
Haupakea
Kamuliwai
Keanaakaluahine (cave)
Kealahula
Kalaeopueo

SECTION 24
Konouli
Kaailana

Nomilu
Awaawalua
Kaponiponi
Oihana
Hanakamanene (1)
Hanakamanene (2)
Kapuaiioale
Kapaleilei
Kalaoa
Honuaula
Kuaakamaku
Waiapuaa
Kamailewalewa
Papailoa
Kumaikaula
Paia

Following are the inland names. They correspond to a line drawn between the letters of their respective sections, A to A, B to B, etc., on the map. The order of their placement follows the direction of the arrow between the letters.

SECTION A
Puili
Nohonohoapola
Kamapuna
Kuahine
Kalaalaau
Waihonu
Waiaohiki
Halalii (koeli)
Mao (paniu)
Kahanuonaihu
Anakii
Keanopua
Wailana
Apuahulihonu
Kahakuku
Laemilo
Kahuelaau
Waikai

Kaunuakala
Waiu
Punawaione
Keonehua
Keanakekolo
Nahaleakaohai
Nuane
Mahu
Alielieokawainui

SECTION B
Napuuhalelua
Puuainako
Kealaikahiki
Kaluaaki
Kialaa
Kamooloa
Popolonui
Ainamaka
Kahekawaiauau

Kawaihapai
Kanahanui
Kanahaiki
Pohakuloa
Kohepahu
Koanui
Moelea
Puapuakea
Apana
Puakaio
Keanopua
Kaakakai
Kauapalehua
Kaluakea
Kapaainahou
Kahalekua
Maulu
Hauhele
Kapaohai

Hanakoa
Kamoilii
Mahu
Papahale
Ohia
Kalaumaki
Panopano
Kulaakapueo
Kaluawauke
Halulu
Kaluaakikoi
Halulukula
Poleho
Pohakuhoee

SECTION C
Umiumipau
Kapohakau
Kapaalalea
Namahana
Pohakuloa
Noni
Panaewa
Kaluawai
Keaki
Kaluaokahuhu
Koiahi
Hiilaau
Kuamanuunuu
Kaluaokuehu
Hamahamo
Kaluaakauwila
Kalawaonui
Kalawaoiki
Pulama
Makalii
Kiekie (home)
Kuhenui
Awanui
Panene
Kiholuwia
Kulai
Keanapahu

Puulehua
Keanaiwila
Keanamanu
Kaenapahoa
Kuikui

SECTION D
Kaluaolohe
Kawaha
Kamoku
Kaleipohina
Kaluanui
Halahala
Waiakeakua

SECTION E
Kalaeloa
Puleole
Puukaioe
Pohina
Hiikeiki
Alimoa
Kamooloa
Kapilepelepe
Kalaihi
Puhala
Kalokoakahina
Nalopapanui
Palenanui
Naaunui
Kamahina
Uwalakaa
Nahaleakeketo
Kawaewae
Lepopalapala
Palianehoa
Mamaua
Kaauwaalua
Kapili
Kaaiea
Kapua
Kalapulehu
Aliaiki
Keanaloa

SECTION F
Onea
Puako
Puaohai
Makalii
Amakakeiki
Kou
Mauuloa
Mauuhaawe
Oneheehee
Aokailio
Kolea
Nanaikauwai
Nanaikoolau
Papakiekie

SECTION G
The 5 Ulu Trees
Hikinaakala
Kulimoku
Hakaleleaponi
Kalama
Nauluhuaikahapapa
Kanakamoli
Kou
Kalaeloa
Apu

SECTION H
Kakakalua (pukapa)
Keahua
Mauupapa
Kulanakoeho
Kelo
Puukoali
Kilomai (punawai)
Humuhumunui
Kaulaakamaka
Makole
Haleakapuolo
Kalama
Kaluamalu
Waiakekohe
Nanauku

MAP INDEX

Kamilo
Kawaikapu (punawai)
Kanuiouka
Makamakaole
Hinapua
Kiamaula
Punikahea
Kupalahao
Kumukalua
Puulepo
Moonui
Mooiki
Palauhulu
Kulaohai
Wiliwilinui
Hanahiona
Kaaneapaa
Kalawaia
Keawaawa
Hanakaalalea
Puakamalii
Loia (kihapai mahiai)
Palawai
Kuuole
Kaniolo
Kaneao
Kuailio
Pilimoo
Mokupapa
Kanaele
Kuhiau
Hoolono
Kauahi

SECTION I

Halekamahina
Napunawaikipapa
Kaioe
Hinamili
Umeumeluahale
Wehekaohu
Ninewa
Haikikala
Keomakani

Kalaekahi
Halaulani
Keanoawaawaa
Poopalani
Uwahi
Kapukaakoolau
Kuamio
Ulumaauea
Kuaapoho
Kahopeakoolau
Kukapoli
Kukalepo
Kou
Kipapa
Kipipi
Makahauena (pukapa)

SECTION J

Kanaana
Puhala
Halekukalahala
Namahana
Kumau
Kapalili
Kukalepe
Kawi
Kaukaopua
Naninaiwa
Kanehala
Kahalepaakea
Hanamili
Kaunuakapu
Peeoe
Kuamoo
Makaokaihe
Palulu
Kaholua
Kealu
Kaunuakala
Haleakala
Kapuaikahi
Pohai kii
Kaluaalilea
Kawaieli (punawai)

Kalenaiki
Kalanikapae
Kahaleakaia
Waikaheka (punawai)
Kuaihala
Noholua
Puhala
Waikomo
Kamoku
Kukahi
Pohakukuai
Kaholua
Niukahi
Halekahi
Kakaimalo
Kapunawaiokou
Kiahamoo
Kalaeloa
Hakikua
Pohakuloa
Kaahupuna
Kapipi (punawai)
Kapili (punawai)
Kamau Kalakahi
Kalaekii (kiionioni)
Wailana
Kamohio
Kahaipu
Halehaa
Kanaele
Kipohopoho
Kalaekiloia
Paa
Kapili
Waiaka (ani kamakani)
Kauanaulu
Puuwaialoha
Naulu
Kauakinikini
Home Iubile

SECTION K

Kaumakani
Halepua

Waiomina
Kepopolo (punawai)
Waiui (punawai)
Waialoha (punawai)
Kuahine
Kaliuwaa
Naniahiahi
Puahinahina
Kaliula
Keaona (punawai)
Palu
Kaluahonu
Hapuuhale
Moenaanune
Haka
Pao
Hopeole
Haaheo
Papakaale (punawai)
Kalokoapio
Kaluawahanui
Kahoolawe
Maleka
Pukaiti (punawai)
Manienie
Kuohai
Pakeehana
Kaluakao
Halemanuahi
Puainako
Halealii
Kahoiwai
Puhikula
Kapunawaieli

SECTION L
Kapuu
Kapoopoo
Ohaiki (punawai)
Kuohai
Kalua
Noni
Kahuamoa
Kihapai

Kaholoakai
Makue
Waiakekalana
Kahaluna
Kapapawai
Pahua
Hoomoewale

SECTION M
Halehaka
Holoipiapia
Ulakoeho
Kaluawauke
Makaleho
Kupahoa
Kaanekiina

SECTION N
Maloeloe
Wailuahale
Keaku
Palipaakea
Kanaele
Kaakohi
Maunaanuanu
Keanahololo
Keahua
Kapuahiokaupo
Maunaaleo
Kaluaakapae
Kaluakahua
Kalihilihiea
Aukila
Palikiiakamoo
Ahailoa
Pohakuakamaile
Holonaakapuaa
Paninaakailio
Hailepo
Kahailoa
Puuohawaii
Kahainuu
Mooakoko
Puehu
Kapuai (hale)

Kalokoakaha
Poahaone
Kauwawea
Alapa
Koenaha (hale)
Hanakealia
Kaluanui
Nanaikoolau (2)
Keanapueo
Keanaakailio
Keanakoa
Pahehoolua
Puulehihi
Kapihe

SECTION O
Keanaohaao
Kanamanu
Kelaokuikui
Haulakuli
Kaumuhonu
Keapauka
Alaohaua
Nenee
Waiaokaikai
Keanaouhi
Kuheanui
Kealaweo
Keanahunaonalii
Kaoleole
Pohueloa
Kukaiaiki
Kukaianui
Kaalialinui
Kawaimakamakahou
Kanaloiki
Kanalo
Waiakanaio
Nianiau
Makaowia
Palina
Puualala
Kahilinei
Kapaka

Kamalu
Waialauki

SECTION P

Waimae
Laeokahiki
Kamanupilau
Waiahelo
Puuuwala
Paele
Nanaikauwai (2)
Kaluaponiu (punawai)
Waiakeakua
Waikea

SECTION Q

Kaalipuaa
Kaaliwai
Kaalihala
Kekelahewaa

Paniau (kilo)
Kepaokanaloiki
Puuiki
Pahupu
Puu Kuikui
Kalamaula
Nanaikeakuli
Pakilehua
Waiahulei
Koolaukani
Kamalukii
Kalapakai
Kalapauka
Palaonui
Puniakapo
Kamahakahaka
Kahoolapa
Konouli
Puulua

Puukahi
Waiauunu
Kalaialamea
Kauneki
Kaoheoku
Wahinemoo
Namahana
Kapahala
Kapauhini
Puhia
Kaeonui
Kaeoiki
Kaoleole
Kamahina
Haahaakawaewae
Makanikoaniani (dam)
Pahupu
Moelea

Island of Niihau

Kauai County, Hawaii

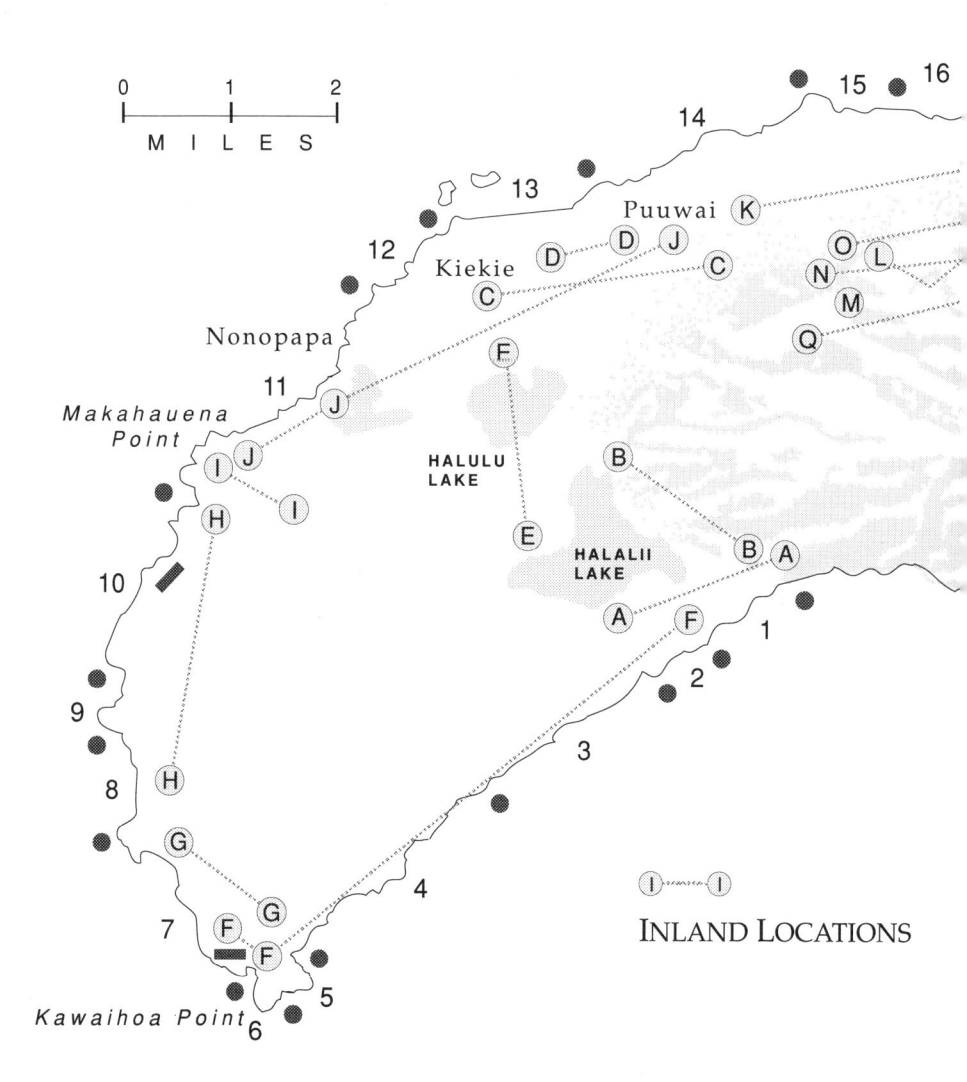

0 1 2 MILES

Puuwai
Kiekie
Nonopapa
Makahauena Point
HALULU LAKE
HALALII LAKE
Kawaihoa Point

Inland Locations

131

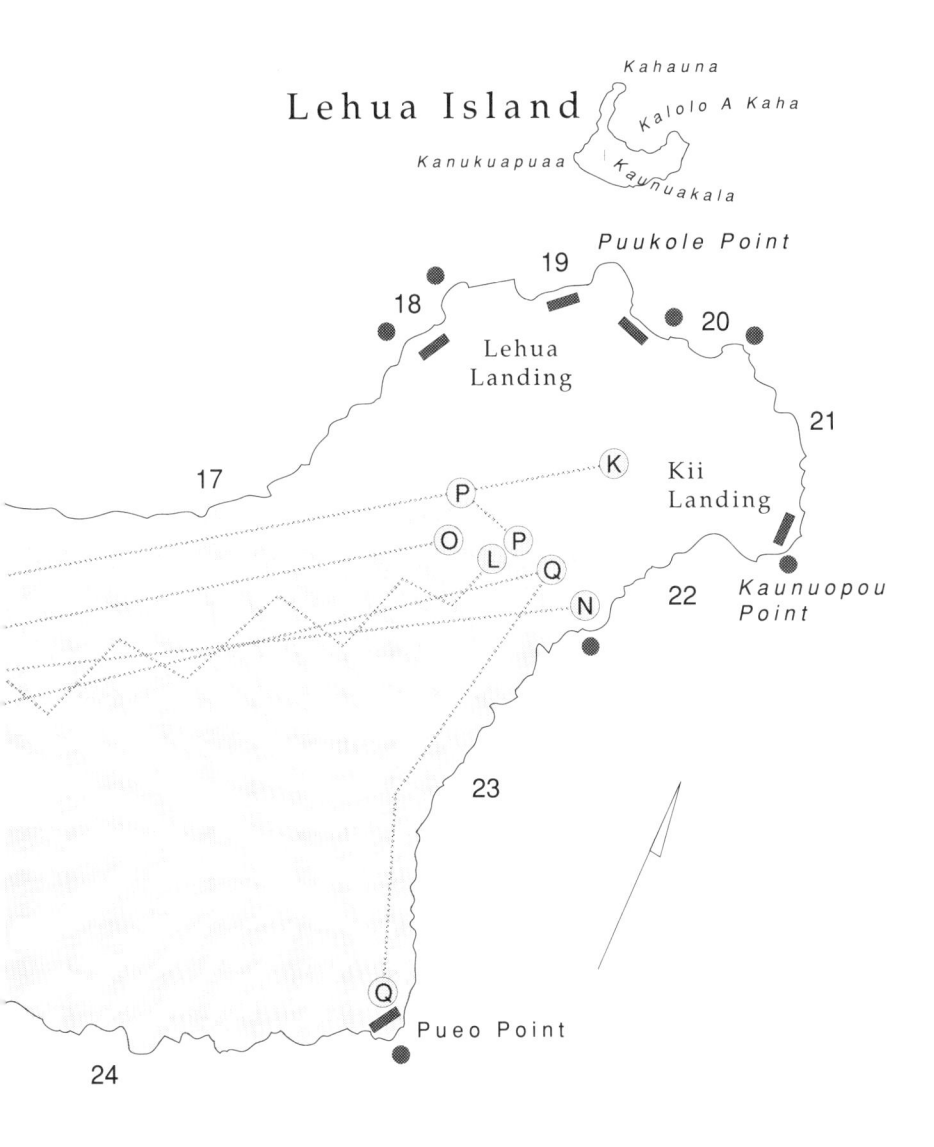

Lehua Island

Kahauna
Kalolo A Kaha
Kanukuapuaa
Kaunuakala

Puukole Point

18
19
20
Lehua Landing
21
17
K
P
Kii Landing
O
L P
Q
N
22
Kaunuopou Point
23

Q
Pueo Point
24

● 2 ●
COASTAL LOCATIONS

▬
HEIAU LOCATIONS

INDEX

agriculture 25
amusements 38
artifacts 30

beaches 88, 90, 91, 93
Beckwith, M. 22
bees 60
Bishop Museum 35
Bolton, H. 65
bows and arrows 32
burials 14, 15, 31

cactus 63
candies 63
canoes 33, 85, 91, 92
cats 63
cattle 63
census 46, 54
channels 93
chants *See mele*
charcoal 6
churches 6, 50, 51
coconut oil 38
Cook, Captain J. 15, 21, 43, 45, 89
crafts 33

daggers 32
daily life 6
December 7, 1941 54
demigod (*kupua*) 20
dogs 46, 63

ehu 45
electricity 7
emigration 18, 46, 51
Emory, Dr. Kenneth 31

Farrington, Wallace R. 37
fishing 64
fishhooks 63
floating logs 33
flowers 63

Gay, George S. 84
geneology
    place names 84
    reference to gods 96
geology 4
goats 45
gourd (*ipu*) 33
grasses
    pili 38, 72
    makiukiu 31, 38

Haka 77
Halemanuahi 77
Hale o paweo 84
Halii 100
halakahiti pineapples 60
halawela 47
Halalii (chief) 13, 18
Halalii (lake) 66, 95
Halulu (chief) 13
Halulu (lake) 4, 34, 66, 95
Hatipohue 94
hee (octopus) 65
hei (string figures) 39
heiau (temples)
    Kahalekuamano 12
    Kaunuakapua 12, 77
    Kaunuohiki 12, 77
    Kaunuokaha 12
    Kaunupou (Koa) 12
    Kauwaha 13

Pahau 13
Pueo 12
Puhiula 13
helua (self-defense) 32, 77, 78, 79
hidden islands (*hunamotu*) 21, 22
Hinds, Norman 4, 32
hipa (sheep) 4, 63, 64
history 3
honu 21
hoohelua 38
Hookano, Kauhi 51
Hoomana Ia Iesu 51
Hualele 39
Hualele 39
hula 17-19
Hunamana, Keala 54
hunamotu (hidden islands) 21, 22
hymns 5, 6, 50

ihe (spear) 32
imu (oven. Also *umu*) 27
ipu (gourd) 33
Iubile Church 51, 52

Kaailana 78
Kaali Cliffs 72
Kaahakakila
  Emma 54
  Kalimahuluhulu 54, 92
Kaahumanu 3, 49, 62, 102
Kaeo 86, 101
Kaeokulani 13, 14, 86, 101
Kahalauwaa 89
Kahekili 14
Kahelelani
  king 13
  shells 36
Kahale, Ed 52, 53
Kaholonakaupena 88
Kaholuana 38
Kaiwimoionakupuna 84
Kalalau 46, 51, 79
Kalanei 67
Kalanihale 89

Kalanimoku 49
Kalaniwai 89
Kalehua 77, 94
Kaleiohano, Hauwila 54
Kaluaakona 52, 85
Kaluaamalu 35
Kaluaapuhi 89
Kaluakahua 84
Kaluakawila 11
Kaluawaiokamakani 95
Kamala, Olivia 13
Kamalino 26, 52, 85, 87
Kamapuaa 71
Kamehameha III 64
Kamehameha IV 46, 47
Kamehameha V 8, 47
Kamoamoa 39
Kanahele
  Ben 55
  Blossom 55
  Kahakuloa 54
  Malaki 54
  Mileka 37
Kanehunamotu 21
Kaoahi 13, 14
Kaohelaulii
  Akana 54
  Enoka 54
  Kekuhina 54
  Willie 54
Kaomea 52
Kapahee nui 12, 79
Kapahee, John 50
Kapahu, Shima 51
Kapapakiikii 85
Kapena Kuke 45, 89
Kapu, Reverend Sam 37
Kapuaiokana 89
Kauai 18, 21, 45, 71
Kauanaulu 79
Kauanaulu (town) 5, 85
Kaula 11, 66, 88, 100
Kaumualii, King 14
Kaumuhonu 35, 85, 89

Kaunu 18
Kaunuakala 100
Kaunuakane 89
Kaununui 48, 67, 90
Kaunuapua 77
Kawahamana 38, 74
Kawaihoa (chief) 13, 38, 64
Kawaihoa (mountain) 13, 22, 26, 38, 49
Kealaakaopihi 102
Keale
   Jean Kelly 55
   Kaaneiikawahaale 22, 51, 84
   Kalua, M.W.K. 75, 84, 88, 92
Keamoai
   Keola Kauiolehua xi, 15, 22, 65, 71, 85, 91
   Kaua 54
   Laeanui 39
Keanaakoko 34
Keanahaki 52, 64, 85, 90
Keanahio 90
Keanamoi 100
Keananoio 85, 100
Keanaoku 74, 101
Keanapou 91
Keanaulii 95
Keaukuu 88
Keikiakamanawa 91
kiawe charcoal 6
Kie Kie 48, 91
Kihawahine 84
Kii 35, 60, 77, 85, 91
Kimo 14
King, Charles E. 37
kinikini (marbles) 38
Knusden, Valdemar 47, 48, 79
ko (sugar cane) 59
Koelilimaohalalii 59
Koakanu, Iosia 47, 48
Koialaau 73
Koia uka 73
Konahina 91
Kuailua *See Helua*

Kuakealii 85
Kuhaimoana 21, 74, 101
Kukaiaiki 21, 99
Kupoloula 14, 40
kupua (demigod) 20
Kuwalu 71

laau (medicine) 60
laau (trees) 62
Laka 18
Lana 38, 74
Lanaikahiki 74
Lanakila 51, 52, 85
language (*olelo*) xii, 5, 15
lava 4
legends 70
Lehu 20
Lehua 21, 99
Leiakauhane 92
lei
   shell 36
   seed 37
limpet (*opihi*) 101
Lonopapa 92
lua See Helua
Luahiwa 74

Makaohina 11
Makalii 14, 86
Makanikahao River 51
mano (shark) 21
Manokalanipo 13, 14, 86
Manoopupaipai 14
maps *See Map Index*
marbles (*kinikini*) 38
mats
   makaloa 15, 34
   neki 34
   tohetohe 34
medicines (*laau*) 60
mele (song, chant) 12, 19, 30, 37, 39, 50, 65, 83, 87
Mikiki, Laisa 54
Minihaha 54

moena mat 15, 34
months of the year 5
moo (lizard) 20
Motupapa 11
Motupapapa 11
Mu 78, 90
mullet ponds
   Halalii 66, 95
   Halulu 4, 34, 66, 95
   Kalanei 67
   Kaununui 48, 67, 90
music *See Afterword*

Naalehu 92
Nakanakaalualikai 92
Nauluhuaikahapapa 26, 71
navigation 12, 79
Nishikaichi, Shigenori 54
Niau, Hannah 53
Niheu, Miriam H. 53
Nihoa 11, 12, 101, 102
Niihauiki 86
Nohokula, Piilani 57, 75
Nonopapa 49, 50, 86, 92
Nualolo 18, 46

octopus (*hee*) 65
octopus lure 65
Ohia 38
olelo (language) xii, 5, 15
oopu, paoo 67
opae (shrimp) 67
opihi (limpet) 101
onions 45
oven (*imu*. Also *umu*) 27
O Waimea Church 50
owl (*pueo*) 21

Paepaeohiiaka 11, 96
Paepaekapuoliloa 88, 96
paakai (salt) 27
Pahauiki 75
Pahaunui 75
Pakehoolua 76

palaoa 15, 31
Palikahea 92
Paniau 86
paoo, oopu 67
Papohaku 14, 86
pawehe
   mats 34
   gourds 33
Paweo 52, 85
peacocks (*pikake*) 64
Pele 11, 18
Peleiholani, Liwai 54
petroglyphs 35
Pewahiuiaakekuawalu 92
pig (*puaa*) 45, 63
pig hunting 63
pikake (peacocks) 64
pili See grasses
Pilikua 76
pineapples 60
Piokeanuenue 86
plants and vegetables 62
poetic sayings 16, 29, 35
pokeokeo (turkeys) 63
Poliolehua 11
Pomakai, Akaneki 54
prayer (*pule*) 7, 53
puaa (pig) 45, 63
pueo (owl) 21
Puhiula 75
pukiawe 37
pule (prayer) 7, 53
pumpkin 45
punawai (water spring) 94
Pupulenalena 71
pupumoeone 84
Puuohawaii 86
Puuone 39
Puwalu 13, 14
Puuwai 5, 52, 94

rabbits 99
religion 50
Robinson

INDEX

Alika 54
Alymer 14, 34
Aubry 4, 6, 14, 49, 59
Lester 63
Salowana 54
Rodman, Julius 14
rope 31
Rowell, Rev. George 47
royal patent *See Appendix*

salt (*paakai*) 27
school 53, 55
seals 67
self-defense (*helua*) 32, 77, 78, 79
shark (*mano*) 21
sheep (*hipa*) 4, 63, 64
shells
　land 37
　ocean 7, 36
　pearl 31
Shintani
　Abigail 55
　Ishimatsu 60
shrimp (*opae*) 67
Sinclair
　Francis 47, 48
　James 47, 48
　Eliza McHutchenson 47, 49
Sinoto, Y.H. Dr. 31
songs *See mele*
spear (*ihe*) 32
string figures (*hei*) 39
sugar cane (*ko*) 59
surfing 38, 39
sweet potato (*uwala, uala*) 25

Tahiti 11, 12, 32, 35, 45, 74, 75, 79, 85

Tahitimoe 86
taro 79
tattoo 45
taxation 3
television 7
temples *See heiau*
Three Aikanaka 76
Tipapa 87
tohola 67
tools 31
trees (*laau*) 62
turkeys (*pokeokeo*) 63

ulu 26
uhi (yams) 27, 45
Unulani 22
Unulau 22
uwala, uala (sweet potato) 25, 45

valleys 87
voting 7

Waiakaulili 95
Waiahole 92
Waiakanaio 95
Waihunaakapaoo 100
Waikai 95
Waikulu 95, 100
water spring (*punawai*) 94
water sources 5, 94
weapons 32
winds 27

yams (*uhi*) 27, 45

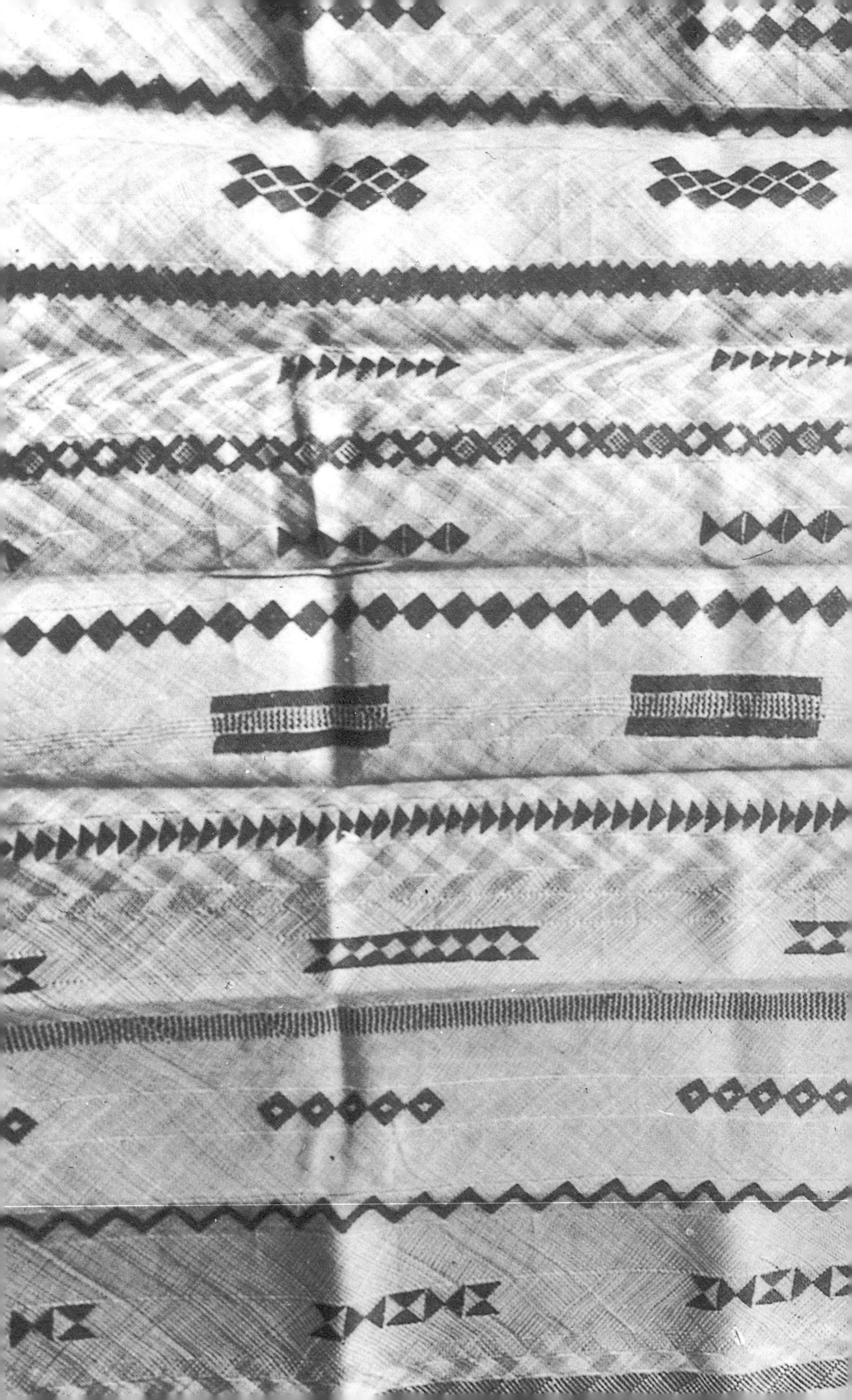